Presented to

_____

From

_____

On this Occasion

_____

On this Date

_____

Reasons for Hope

Reasons for Hope
Holding onto God's Promises

Compiled by Voletta Ann Hays

PINTEGRITY PRESS ™
Reasons for Hope – Holding onto God's Promises
Copyright © 2016, compiled by Voletta Ann Hays
All rights Reserved

ISBN 0990919811
ISBN 13: 9780990919810

Scripture quotations marked AKJV are taken from the American King James Version of
the Bible, http://WWW.angelfire.com/a14/allenkc/akjv/, published in 1999. (Accessed
April 23, 2013)

Scripture quotations marked WEB are taken from the World English Bible, modern
English translation, http://WWW.biblegateway.com/versions/World-English-Bible-
WEB/, New Testament version, published in 2000. (Accessed March 6, 2014.)

Scripture quotations marked CPDV are taken from the Catholic Public Domain
Version of the Sacred Bible, modern translation from the Latin Vulgate, http:WWW.
sacredbible.org/catholic/version.htm, published in 2009. (Accessed April 9, 2013)

Scripture quotations marked NHEB are taken from the Holy Bible, New Heart English
Bible, http://studybible.info/version/NHEB. New Testament with Psalms and Proverbs,
Publication 2010. (Accessed March 6, 2014)

I am indebted to the artists who put their works of art out for all to enjoy. Listed in order of appearance:

ZoranKrstic/Shutterstock.com

Nejron Photo/Shutterstock.com

Chris Humphries/Shutterstock.com

Andy Lim/Shutterstock.com

Luis Zapico/Shutterstock.com

Eric Stock Media/Shutterstock.com

Mjoseph92/Shutterstock.com

Scubaluna/Shutterstock.com

Dmitry Kulagin/Shutterstock.com

Michael Warwick/Shutterstock.com

Max Topchii/Shutterstock.com

Treasured dragon/Shutterstock.com

Bjonesphotography/Shutterstock.com

Vadim Petrakov/Shutterstock.com

Kucher Serhii/Shutterstock.com

Dmitry Rukhlenko/Shutterstock.com

Tischenko Irina/Shutterstock.com

Manop/Shutterstock.com

Ileana_bt/Shutterstock.com

Nutkamol Komolvanich/Shutterstock.com

Furtseff/Shutterstock.com

BMJ/Shutterstock.com

Aaron Amat/Shutterstock.com

Mark Heighes/Shutterstock.com

Izz Hazel/Shutterstock.com

Elena Dijour/Shutterstock.com

Tuahlensa/Shutterstock.com

TheOldhiro/Shutterstock.com

Ellerslie/Shutterstock.com

Introduction

$\mathcal{L}$et me see now, where should I begin? How about: CONGRATULATIONS! Here you are and here is a book of promises. You picked this book up for a reason. Why? What was your first thought? Was it the title? Was it for knowledge? Was it for peace of mind? Or could it be that you just need a little hope in the lean times?

They say, whoever they are, behind every good book lies a story. I guess mine began with the thought that there are people out there, who do not believe in a god, not to mention Jesus Christ. What keeps them going? And when they get there, wherever they are going, what motivates his or her next move? I remember the difficulties in my life before I became a Christian. Maybe someday I will tell you about it. That is a story in itself.

So as an adult I became a believer, right? But I didn't know where to find the information to feed my ever-hungry spirit. I had so many questions. I did not grow up in a Christian home. It was every man for himself, so-to-speak. So one day I picked up a Bible – the old King James Version. Wow, I didn't know I needed to take a lesson in the art of Shakespeare! I couldn't figure out how to pronounce or understand what I was reading, which at times brought on more questions than answers. To make a long story short, I eventually thumbed my way through a few bibles and quickly learned what The Lord wanted me to know, in His timing. Go figure.

It can be difficult for a new believer to hold onto hope, especially when things go wrong and you're still not quite sure where or how to turn. After all, you have been your own god, for the most part. Which reminds me: never, I repeat, never, let a new believer start reading at Revelation. There again, is a chapter in my life that we can pick up some other time.

I have compiled these verses with new believers in mind, but this book will be an inspiration to all. Many of the verses are from the New Testament, the place where a new believer is likely to begin his or her journey into scripture. However; I have found myself being drawn to the Psalms and Proverbs many times. Thus I have included some of these verses, as well, since they are very fitting for this purpose.

There are times when security and hope can be a bumpy ride. It is a ride that only God can guide us through and smooth out; we need only to ask Him to fulfill our needs and desires. He wants us to come to Him. Isn't it funny that when we become adults, we forget how to ask for help? Most of us had no problem asking for help when we were children. So I guess my message is this: it is my hope that you gain hope because our Lord certainly has Hope to give. Through His Word, we can find peace and in His faithful, generous arms, He loves on us and gives us hope.

I simply want to encourage you. I want to give you something to reflect on. But most of all, I want to give you Reasons for Hope.

Contents

Be of good cheer; I have
Overcome the World.

There are Reasons for Hope

⚜

Now may the God of hope fill you with all joy and peace in believing, that you may abound in hope, in the power of the Holy Spirit.

Romans 15:13 NHEB

According to the foreknowledge of God the Father, in sanctification of the Spirit, that you may obey Jesus Christ and be sprinkled with his blood: Grace to you and peace be multiplied.

1 Peter 1:2 NHEB

Blessed be the God and Father of our Lord Jesus Christ, who according to his great mercy became our father again to a living hope through the resurrection of Jesus Christ from the dead.

1 Peter 1:3 WEB

For to this end we both labor and strive, because we have set our trust in the living God, who is the Savior of all men, especially of those who believe.

1 Timothy 4:10

For whatever things were written before were written for our learning, that through patience and through encouragement of the Scriptures we might have hope.

Roman 15:4 CPDV

But let us, who are of the day, be sober, putting on the breastplate of faith and love; and for a helmet, the hope of salvation.

1 Thessalonians 5:8 AKJV

Remembering your work of faith, and hardship, and charity, and enduring hope, in our Lord Jesus Christ, before God our Father.

1 Thessalonians 1:3 NHEB

If we have only hoped in Christ in this life, we are of all men most pitiable.

1 Corinthians 15:19 WEB

May the eyes of your heart be illuminated, so that you may know what is the hope of his calling, and the wealth of the glory of his inheritance with the saint.

Ephesians 1:18 CPDV

Because of the hope which is laid up for you in the heavens, of which you heard before in the word of the truth of the Good News.

Colossians 1:5 WEB

Now our Lord Jesus Christ himself, and God our Father, who loved us and gave us eternal comfort and good hope through grace, comfort your hearts and establish you in every good work and word.

2 Thessalonians 2:16-17 WEB

Looking for the blessed hope and appearing of the glory of our great God and Savior, Jesus Christ.

Titus 2:13 WEB

So that, having been justified by his grace, we may become heirs according to the hope of eternal life

Titus 3:7 CPDV

We desire that each one of you may show the same diligence to the fullness of hope even to the end.

Hebrews 6:11 NHEB

That by two immutable things, in which it is impossible for God to lie, we may have a strong encouragement, who have fled for refuge to take hold of the hope set before us. This hope we have as an anchor of the soul, a hope both sure and steadfast and entering into that which is within the veil.

Hebrews 6:18-19 NHEB

(For the law made nothing perfect), and a bringing in of a better hope, through which we draw near to God.

Hebrews 7:19 NHEB

Everyone who has this hope set on him purifies himself, even as he is pure.

1 John 3:3 NHEB2

And hope doesn't disappoint us, because God's love has been poured out into our hearts through the Holy Spirit who was given to us.

Romans 5:5 WEB

To whom God was pleased to make known what are the riches of the glory of this mystery among the Gentiles, which is Christ in you, the hope of glory.

Colossians 1:27 TWEB

Therefore prepare your minds for action, be sober, and set your hope fully on the grace that will be brought to you at the revelation of Jesus Christ.

1 Peter 1:13 WEB

Rejoicing in hope; enduring in troubles; continuing steadfastly in prayer.

Romans 12:12 WEB

And in his name, the nations will hope.

Matthew 12:21 WEB

Now may the God of hope fill you with all joy and peace in believing, that you may abound in hope, in the power of the Holy Spirit.

Romans 15:13 NHEB

Wait for the LORD. Be strong, and let your heart take courage. Yes, wait for the LORD.

Psalm 27:14 NHEB

But you brought me out of the womb. You made me trust at my mother's breasts.

Psalm 22:9 NHEB

Behold, the LORD's eye is on those who fear him, on those who hope in his loving kindness; to deliver their soul from death, to keep them alive in famine. Our soul has waited for the LORD. He is our help and our shield. For our heart rejoices in him, because we have trusted in his holy name. Let your loving kindness be on us, LORD, since we have hoped in you.

Psalm 33:18-22 NHEB

Now, Lord, what do I wait for? My hope is in you.

Psalm 39:7 NHEB

Be strong, and let your heart take courage, all you who hope in the LORD.

Psalm 31:24 NHEB

Why are you in despair, my soul? Why are you disturbed within me? Hope in God! For I shall still praise him for the saving help of his presence.

Psalm 42:5 NHEB

Why are you in despair, my soul? Why are you disturbed within me? Hope in God! For I shall still praise him, the saving help of my countenance, and my God.

Psalm 42:11 NHEB

For you are my hope, Lord GOD; my confidence from my youth.

Psalm 71:5 NHEB

The prospect of the righteous is joy, but the hope of the wicked will perish.

Proverbs 10:28 NHEB

When a wicked man dies, hope perishes, and expectation of power comes to nothing.

Proverbs 11:7 NHEB

Hope deferred makes the heart sick, but when longing is fulfilled, it is a tree of life.

Proverbs 13:12 NHEB

The wicked is brought down in his calamity, but in death, the righteous has a refuge.

Proverbs 14:32 NHEB

Discipline your son, for there is hope; do not be a willing party to his death.

Proverbs 19:18 NHEB

Do you see a man wise in his own eyes? There is more hope for a fool than for him.

Proverb 26:12 NHEB

Do you see a man who is hasty in his words? There is more hope for a fool than for him.

Proverbs 29:20 NHEB

NOTES

Jesus is my Everything

*To everything there is a season, and a
time to every purpose under heaven.*

ECCLESIASTES

❖

All things, whatever you ask in prayer, believing, you will receive.

Matthew 21:22 NHEB

If you remain in me, and my words remain in you, you will ask whatever you desire, and it will be done for you.

John 15:7 WEB

Until now, you have asked nothing in my name. Ask, and you will receive, that your joy may be made full.

John 16:24 NHEB

Therefore I tell you, all things whatever you pray and ask for, believe that you have received them, and you shall have them.

Mark 11:24 NHEB

Blessed be the God and Father of our Lord Jesus Christ, who has blessed us with every spiritual blessing in the heavenly places in Christ.

Ephesians 1:3 WEB

And whatever we ask, we receive from him, because we keep his commandments and do the things that are pleasing in his sight.

1 John 3:22 WEB

Therefore let no one boast in men. For all things are yours, whether Paul, or Apollos, or Cephas, or the world, or life, or death, or things present, or things to come. All are yours, and you are Christ's, and Christ is God's

1 Corinthians 3:21-23 WEB

I can do all things through Christ, who strengthens me.

Philippians 4:13 WEB

My God will supply every need of yours according to his riches in glory in Christ Jesus.

Philippians 4:19 WEB

For to me to live is Christ, and to die is gain.

Philippians 1:21 NHEB

No, in all these things, we are more than conquerors through him who loved us.

Romans 8:37 WEB

For the law of the Spirit of life in Christ Jesus made me free from the law of sin and of death.

Romans 8:2 WEB

For him who knew no sin he made to be sin on our behalf; so that in him we might become the righteousness of God.

2 Corinthians 5:21 WEB

Therefore if anyone is in Christ, he is a new creation. The old things have passed away. Behold, all things have become new.

2 Corinthians 5:17 WEB

And God is able to make all grace abound to you, that you, always having all sufficiency in everything, may abound to every good work.

2 Corinthians 9:8 NHEB

"You will know the truth, and the truth will make you free." If therefore the Son makes you free, you will be free indeed.

John 8:32, 36 WEB

Blessed are they which do hunger and thirst after righteousness: for they shall be filled.

Matthew 5:6 AKJV

Jesus Christ is the same yesterday, today, and forever.

Hebrews 13:8 WEB

I will be to you a Father. You will be to me sons and daughters,' says the Lord Almighty."

2 Corinthians 6:18 NHEB

NOTES

He is the Lord

He says not, 'at the end of the way you find
Me.' He says, 'I AM the way: I AM
the road under your feet, the road that
begins just as low as you happen to be.'

ANONYMOUS

✦

Therefore God also highly exalted him, and gave to him the name which is above every name; that at the name of Jesus every knee should bow, of those in heaven, those on earth, and those under the earth, and that every tongue should confess that Jesus Christ is Lord, to the glory of God the Father.

Philippians 2:9-11 WEB

Behold, I stand at the door and knock. If anyone will hear my voice and will open the door to me, I will enter to him, and I will dine with him, and he with me.

Revelation 3:20 CPDV

"That if you will confess with your mouth that Jesus is Lord, and believe in your heart that God raised him from the dead, you will be saved. For with the heart, one believes unto righteousness; and with the mouth confession is made unto salvation. For the Scripture says, "Whoever believes in him will not be disappointed."

Romans 10:9-10 WEB

Therefore I urge you, brothers, by the mercies of God, to present your bodies a living sacrifice, holy, acceptable to God, which is your spiritual service. Don't be conformed to this world, but be transformed by the renewing of your mind, so that you may prove what is the good, well-pleasing, and perfect will of God.

Romans 12:1-2 WEB

For if we live, we live to the Lord. Or if we die, we die to the Lord. If therefore we live or die, we are the Lord's.

Romans 14:8 WEB

"Why do you call me, 'Lord, Lord,' and do not do the things which I say?"

Luke 6:46 NHEB

And you shall love the Lord your God from your whole heart, and from your whole soul, and from your whole mind, and from your whole strength. This is the first commandment.

Mark 12:30 CPDV

Or do you not know that your body is a temple of the Holy Spirit which is in you, which you have from God? You are not your own, for you were bought with a price. Therefore glorify God in your body.

1 Corinthians 6:19-20 NHEB

For where two or three are gathered together in my name, there am I in the middle of them.

Matthew 18:20 AKJV

Remain in me, and I in you. As the branch cannot bear fruit by itself, unless it remains in the vine, so neither can you, unless you remain in me. I am the vine. You are the branches. He who remains in me, and I in him, the same bears much fruit, for apart from me you can do nothing. If a man does not remain in me, he is thrown out as a branch, and is withered; and they gather them, throw them into the fire, and they are burned. If you remain in me, and my words remain in you, ask whatever you desire, and it will be done for you.

John 15:4-7 NHEB

"One who has my commandments, and keeps them, that person is one who loves me. One who loves me will be loved by my Father, and I will love him, and will reveal myself to him."

John 14:21 NHEB

"Are not two sparrows sold for an assarion coin? Not one of them falls on the ground apart from your Father's will, but the very hairs of your head are all numbered."

Matthew 10:29-30 NHEB

"What do you think? If a man has one hundred sheep, and one of them goes astray, does he not leave the ninety-nine, go to the mountains, and seek that which has gone astray? If he finds it, truly I tell you, he rejoices over it more than over the ninety-nine which have not gone astray. Even so it is not the will of my Father who is in heaven that one of these little ones should perish."

Matthew 18:12-14 NHEB

All the earth will worship you, and will sing to you; they will sing to your name. Selah.

Psalm 66:4 NHEB

All nations you have made will come and worship before you, Lord. They shall glorify your name.

Psalm 86:9 NHEB

Oh come, let's worship and bow down. Let's kneel before the LORD, our Maker, for he is our God. We are the people of his pasture, and the sheep in his care. Today, oh that you would hear his voice!

Psalm 95:6-7

Make a joyful noise to the LORD, all the earth! Burst out and sing for joy, yes, sing praises!

Psalm 98:4 NHEB

Exalt the LORD our God. Worship at his footstool. He is Holy!

Psalm 99:5 NHEB

Exalt the LORD, our God. Worship at his holy hill, for the LORD, our God, is holy!

Psalm 99:9 NHEB

<A Psalm of thanksgiving.> Shout for joy to the LORD, all you lands!

Psalm 100:1 NHEB

NOTES

He Teaches by Example

*Just as a flower unfolds to take in light, so does
the spirit to knowledge, truth and wisdom.*

V A HAYS

✤

You call me, 'Teacher' and 'Lord.' You say so correctly, for so I am. If I then, the Lord and the Teacher, have washed your feet, you also ought to wash one another's feet. For I have given you an example, that you also should do as I have done to you.

John 13:14-15 WEB

"A new commandment I give to you, that you love one another. Just as I have loved you, you also love one another. By this everyone will know that you are my disciples, if you have love for one another."

John 13:34-35 WEB

For to this you were called, because Christ also suffered for us, leaving you an example, that you should follow his steps.

1 Peter 2:21 WEB

For whatever things were written before were written for our learning, that through patience and through encouragement of the Scriptures we might have hope. Now the God of patience and of encouragement grant you to be of the same mind one with another according to Christ Jesus, that with one accord you may with one mouth glorify the God and Father of our Lord Jesus Christ. Therefore accept one another, even as Christ also accepted you, to the glory of God.

Romans 15:4-7 NHEB

Looking to Jesus, the author and finisher of our faith, who for the joy that was set before him endured the cross, disregarding its shame, and has sat down at the right hand of the throne of God. For consider him who has endured such hostility from sinners against himself, so that you do not grow weary in your souls and lose heart.

Hebrew 12:2-3 NHEB

He who says he remains in him ought himself also to walk just like he walked.

1 John 2:6 NHEB

Every Scripture is God-breathed and profitable for teaching, for reproof, for correction, and for instruction in righteousness.

2 Timothy 3:16 WEB

You call me, 'Teacher' and 'Lord.' You say so correctly, for so I am.

John 13:13 NHEB

But you remain in the things which you have learned and have been assured of, knowing from whom you have learned them. From infancy, you have known the Holy Scriptures which are able to make you wise for salvation through faith, which is in Christ Jesus.

2 Timothy 3:14-15 WEB

I will instruct you and teach you in the way which you shall go. I will counsel you with my eye on you.

Psalm 28:8 NHEB

NOTES

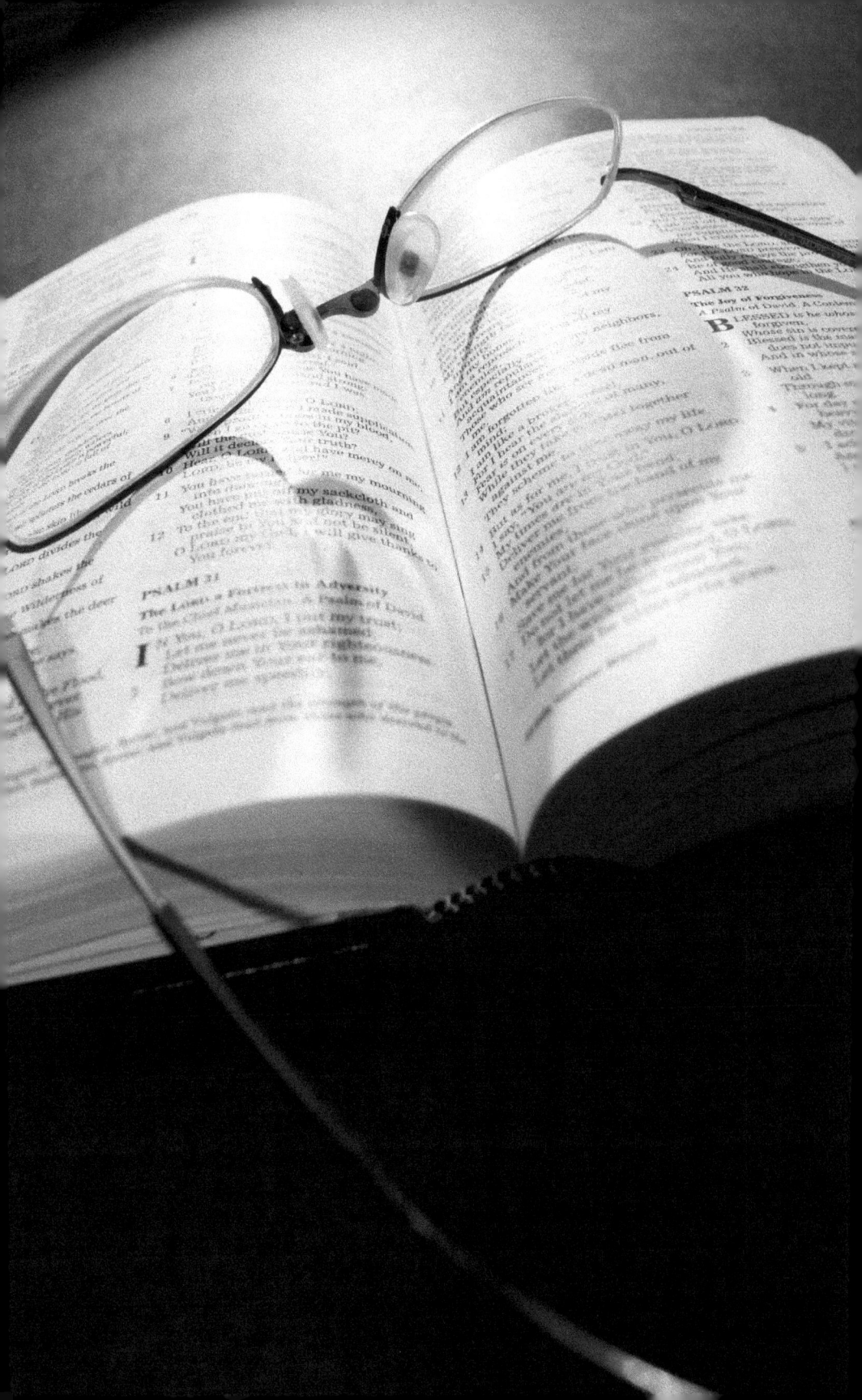

PSALM 32

The Joy of Forgiveness

A Psalm of David. A Cont...

BLESSED is he who...

PSALM 31

The LORD a Fortress in Adversity

Jesus is my Savior

For when the One Great Scorer comes, to write
against your name, He writes not that you
lost or won, but how you played the game.

ANONYMOUS

❖

Not by works of righteousness, which we did ourselves, but according to his mercy, he saved us, through the washing of rebirth and renewing by the Holy Spirit, whom he poured out on us richly, through Jesus Christ our Savior.

Titus 3:5-6 NHEB

Most certainly, I tell you, he who believes in me has eternal life.

John 6:47 WEB

For we have heard him ourselves, and know that this is indeed the Christ, the Savior of the world.

John 4:42 AKJV

For God so loved the world, that he gave his one and only Son, that whoever believes in him should not perish, but have eternal life.

John 3:16 WEB

He who did not spare his own Son, but delivered him up for us all, how would he not also with him freely give us all things?

Romans 8:32 NHEB

That if you will confess with your mouth that Jesus is Lord, and believe in your heart that God raised him from the dead, you will be saved. For with the heart, one believes unto righteousness; and with the mouth confession is made unto salvation.

Romans 10:9-10 NHEB

We have seen and testify that the Father has sent the Son as the Savior of the world. Whoever confesses that Jesus is the Son of God, God remains in him, and he in God.

1 John 4:14-15 NHEB

My spirit has rejoiced in God my Savior.

Luke 1:47 WEB

"For the Son of Man came to seek and to save that which was lost."

Luke 19:10

But God, being rich in mercy, for his great love with which he loved us, even when we were dead through our trespasses, made us alive together with Christ (by grace you have been saved).

Ephesians 2:4-5 WEB

Who saved us and called us with a holy calling, not according to our works, but according to his own purpose and grace, which was given to us in Christ Jesus before times eternal, but has now been revealed by the appearing of our Savior, Christ Jesus, who abolished death, and brought life and immortality to light through the Good News.

2 Timothy 1:9-10 NHEB

For by grace you have been saved through faith, and that not of yourselves; it is the gift of God, not of works, that no one would boast.

Ephesians 2:8-9 NHEB

Therefore if anyone is in Christ, he is a new creation. The old things have passed away. Behold, new things have come.

2 Corinthians 5:17 NHEB

For to this end we both labor and strive, because we have set our trust in the living God, who is the Savior of all men, especially of those who believe.

1 Timothy 4:10 NHEB

Voletta Ann Hays

NOTES

He is my Protection

Fear not the unknown; rather accept it as an adventure.

V A HAYS

❧

My little children, I write these things to you so that you may not sin. If anyone sins, we have an Advocate with the Father, Jesus Christ, the righteous. And he is the atoning sacrifice for our sins, and not for ours only, but also for the whole world.

1 John 2:1-2 NHEB

For I am persuaded, that neither death, nor life, nor angels, nor principalities, nor things present, nor things to come, nor powers, nor height, nor depth, nor any other created thing, will be able to separate us from the love of God, which is in Christ Jesus our Lord.

Romans 8:38-39 NHEB

In whom you also, having heard the word of the truth, the Good News of your salvation,—in whom, having also believed, you were sealed with the Holy Spirit of promise.

Ephesians 1:13 NHEB

Do not grieve the Holy Spirit of God, in whom you were sealed for the day of redemption.

Ephesians 4:30 NHEB

For the eyes of the Lord are on the righteous, and his ears open to their prayer; but the face of the Lord is against those who do evil. Now who is he who will harm you, if you become zealous of that which is good?

1 Peter 3:12-13 NHEB

But the Lord is faithful, who will establish you, and guard you from the evil one.

2 Thessalonians 3:3 WEB

Do not work for the food which perishes, but for the food which remains to eternal life, which the Son of Man will give to you. For God the Father has sealed him.

John 6:27 NHEB

All those whom the Father gives me will come to me. He who comes to me I will in no way throw out. For I have come down from heaven, not to do my own will, but the will of him who sent me.

John 6:37-38 NHEB

In peace I will both lay myself down and sleep, for you, the LORD alone, make me live in safety.

Psalm 4:8 NHEB

The LORD is my light and my salvation. Whom shall I fear? The LORD is the strength of my life. Of whom shall I be afraid?

Psalm 27:1 NHEB

Because you have made LORD your refuge, and the Most High your dwelling place, no evil shall overtake you; no plague shall come near your dwelling.

Psalm 91:9-10 NHEB

He will not be afraid of evil news. His heart is steadfast, trusting in the LORD.

Psalm 112:7 NHEB

The LORD will keep you from all evil. He will keep your soul. The LORD will keep your going out and your coming in, from this time forth, and forevermore.

Psalm 121:7-8 NHEB

But whoever listens to me will dwell securely, and will be at ease, without fear of harm."

Proverb 1:33 WEB

When you lie down, you will not be afraid. Yes, you will lie down, and your sleep will be sweet.

Proverbs 3:24 WEB

Yahweh's name is a strong tower: the righteous run to him, and are safe.

Proverb 18:10 WEB

For in the day of trouble he will keep me secretly in his pavilion. In the covert of his tabernacle he will hide me. He will lift me up on a rock.

Psalm 27:5 NHEB

NOTES

Why be Discouraged or Confused

Life is like a ladder. Every step we take is either up or down.

ANONYMOUS

For where jealousy and selfish ambition are, there is confusion and every evil deed. But the wisdom that is from above is first pure, then peaceful, gentle, reasonable, full of mercy and good fruits, without partiality, and without hypocrisy. Now the fruit of righteousness is sown in peace by those who make peace.

James 3:16-18 WEB

Peace I leave with you. My peace I give to you. I do not give to you as the world gives. Do not let your heart be troubled, neither let it be afraid. You heard how I told you, 'I go away, and I come to you.' If you loved me, you would have rejoiced, because I am going to the Father; for the Father is greater than I.

John 14:27-28 NHEB

But if any of you lacks wisdom, let him ask of God, who gives to all liberally and without reproach; and it will be given to him.

James 1:5 WEB

Being confident of this very thing, that he who began a good work in you will complete it until the day of Jesus Christ.

Philippians 1:6 WEB

In nothing be anxious, but in everything, by prayer and petition with thanksgiving, let your requests be made known to God. And the peace of God, which surpasses all understanding, will guard your hearts and your thoughts in Christ Jesus.

Philippians 4:6-7 WEB

For God didn't give us a spirit of fear, but of power, love, and self-control.

2 Timothy 1:7 WEB

"Don't let your heart be troubled. Believe in God. Believe also in me. In my Father's house are many homes. If it weren't so, I would have told you. I am going to prepare a place for you. If I go and prepare a place for you, I will come again, and will receive you to myself that where I am, you may be there also.

John 14:1-3 WEB

We are pressed on every side, yet not crushed; perplexed, yet not to despair; pursued, yet not forsaken; struck down, yet not destroyed.

2 Corinthians 4:8-9 WEB

Beloved, do not be astonished at the fiery trial which has come upon you, to test you, as though a strange thing happened to you. But because you are partakers of Christ's sufferings, rejoice; that at the revelation of glory you also may rejoice with exceeding joy.

1 Peter 4:12-13 NHEB

Wherein you greatly rejoice, though now for a little while, if need be, you have been put to grief in various trials, that the proof of your faith, which is more precious than gold that perishes even though it is tested by fire, may be found to result in praise, glory, and honor at the revelation of Jesus Christ— whom not having known you love; in whom, though now you don't see him, yet believing, you rejoice greatly with joy unspeakable and full of glory— receiving the result of your faith, the salvation of your souls.

1 Peter 1:6-9 WEB

Therefore don't throw away your boldness, which has a great re-ward. For you need endurance so that, having done the will of God, you may receive the promise.

Hebrews 10:35-36 WEB

NOTES

I am filled with His Love

*Add all the love of all the parents and the total
sum cannot be multiplied enough times to express
God's love for me, the least of His children.*

ANONYMOUS

❦

Jesus said to them, "I am the bread of life. He who comes to me will not be hungry, and he who believes in me will never be thirsty.

John 6:35 WEB

Blessed are those who hunger and thirst for justice, for they shall be satisfied.

Matthew 5:6 CPDV

We know and have believed the love which God has for us. God is love, and he who remains in love remains in God, and God remains in him. In this love has been made perfect among us, that we may have boldness in the Day of Judgment, because as he is, even so are we in this world. There is no fear in love; but perfect love casts out fear, because fear has punishment. He who fears is not made perfect in love. We love him, because he first loved us.

1 John 4:16-19 WEB

Beloved, let us love one another, for love is of God; and everyone who loves is born of God, and knows God. He who does not love does not know God, for God is love. By this God's love was revealed in us, that God has sent his one and only Son into the world that we might live through him. In this is love, not that we have loved God, but that he loved us, and sent his Son as the atoning sacrifice for our sins. Beloved, if God loved us in this way, we also ought to love one another. No one has seen God at any time. If we love one another, God remains in us, and his love has been perfected in us.

1 John 4:7-12 NHEB

But now faith, hope, and love remain—these three. The greatest of these is love.

1 Corinthians 13:13 WEB

For God so loved the world, that he gave his only begotten Son, that whoever believes in him should not perish, but have everlasting life.

John 3:16 KJV

Jesus answered and said to her, Whoever drinks of this water shall thirst again: But whoever drinks of the water that I shall give him shall never thirst; but the water that I shall give him shall be in him a well of water springing up into everlasting life.

John 4:13-14 KJV

Even as the Father has loved me, I also have loved you. Remain in my love. If you keep my commandments, you will remain in my love; even as I have kept my Father's commandments, and remain in his love. I have spoken these things to you, that my joy may remain in you, and that your joy may be made full. "This is my commandment, that you love one another, even as I have loved you. Greater love has no one than this that someone lay down his life for his friends.

John 15:9-13 WEB

One who has my commandments, and keeps them, that person is one who loves me. One who loves me will be loved by my Father, and I will love him, and will reveal myself to him."

John 14:21 WEB

For I am persuaded, that neither death, nor life, nor angels, nor principalities, nor things present, nor things to come, nor powers, nor height, nor depth, nor any other created thing, will be able to separate us from the love of God, which is in Christ Jesus our Lord.

Romans 8:38-39 NHEB

That Christ may dwell in your hearts through faith; to the end that you, being rooted and grounded in love, may be strengthened to comprehend with all the saints what is the width and length and height and depth, and to know Christ's love which surpasses knowledge, that you may be filled with all the fullness of God.

Ephesians 3:17-19 WEB

In this is love, not that we have loved God, but that he loved us, and sent his Son as the atoning sacrifice for our sins.

1 John 4:10 NHEB

But God, being rich in mercy, for his great love with which he loved us, even when we were dead through our trespasses, made us alive together with Christ (by grace you have been saved), and raised us up with him, and made us to sit with him in the heavenly places in Christ Jesus, that in the ages to come he might show the exceeding riches of his grace in kindness toward us in Christ Jesus.

Ephesians 2:4-7

For the Father himself loves you, because you have loved me, and have believed that I came from God.

John 16:27 WEB

"And I have made known your name to them, and I will make it known, so that the love in which you have loved me may be in them, and so that I may be in them."

John 17:26 CPDV

I am in them, and you are in me. So may they be perfected as one. And may the world know that you have sent me and that you have loved them, just as you have also loved me

John 17:23 CPDV

As the Father has loved me, so I have loved you. Abide in my love.

John 15:9 CPDV

But as it is written, "Things which an eye did not see, and an ear did not hear, which did not enter into the heart of man, these God has prepared for those who love him."

1 Corinthians 2:9 NHEB

Grace be with all those who love our Lord Jesus Christ with incorruptible love. Amen.

Ephesians 6:24 WEB

And hope doesn't disappoint us, because God's love has been poured out into our hearts through the Holy Spirit who was given to us.

Romans 5:5 WEB

Now our Lord Jesus Christ himself, and God our Father, who loved us and gave us eternal comfort and good hope through grace, comfort your hearts and establish you in every good work and word.

2 Thessalonians 2:16-17 WEB

I will be to you a Father. You will be to me sons and daughters, says the Lord Almighty."

2 Corinthians 6:18 NHEB

"Before I formed you in the womb, I knew you. Before you were born, I sanctified you. I have appointed you a prophet to the nations."

Jeremiah 1:5 WEB

But as many as received him, to them he gave the right to become God's children, to those who believe in his name.

John 1:12 NHEB

But when Jesus saw it, he was moved with indignation, and said to them, "Allow the little children to come to me! Do not forbid them, for the Kingdom of God belongs to such as these.

Mark 10:14 NHEB

Who shall separate us from the love of Christ? Could oppression, or anguish, or persecution, or famine, or nakedness, or peril, or sword? No, in all these things, we are more than conquerors through him who loved us. For I am persuaded, that neither death, nor life, nor angels, nor principalities, nor things present, nor things to come, nor powers, nor height, nor depth, nor any other created thing, will be able to separate us from the love of God, which is in Christ Jesus our Lord.

Romans 8:35; 8:37-39 NHEB

Have mercy on us, LORD, have mercy on us, for we have endured much contempt.

Psalm 123:3 NHEB

For in the day of trouble he will keep me secretly in his pavilion. In the covert of his tabernacle he will hide me. He will lift me up on a rock.

Psalm 27:5 NHEB

We will not hide them from their children, telling to the generation to come, the praises of the LORD, his strength, and his wondrous works that he has done.

Psalm 78:4 NHEB

Like a father has compassion on his children, so the LORD has compassion on those who fear him.

Psalm 103:13 NHEB

Are not two sparrows sold for one small coin? And yet not one of them will fall to the ground without your Father.

Matthew 10:29 CPDV

How does it seem to you? If someone has one hundred sheep, and if one of them has gone astray, should he not leave behind the ninety-nine in the mountains, and go out to seek what has gone astray? And if he should happen to find it: Amen I say to you, that he has more joy over that one, than over the ninety-nine which did not go astray. Even so, it is not the will before your Father, who is in heaven, that one of these little ones should be lost.

Matthew 18:12-14 CPDV

NOTES

When I feel Alone or Depressed

Life is not a solo but a chorus; we live in relationships from cradle to grave.

ANONYMOUS

✤

Who shall separate us from the love of Christ? Could oppression, or anguish, or persecution, or famine, or nakedness, or peril, or sword? Even as it is written, "For your sake we are killed all day long. We were accounted as sheep for the slaughter." No, in all these things, we are more than conquerors through him who loved us. For I am persuaded, that neither death, nor life, nor angels, nor principalities, nor things present, nor things to come, nor powers, nor height, nor depth, nor any other created thing, will be able to separate us from the love of God, which is in Christ Jesus our Lord.

Romans 8:35-39 NHEB

They cried, and the LORD hears, and delivers them out of all their troubles.

Psalm 34:17 NHEB

"Don't let your heart be troubled. Believe in God. Believe also in me.

John 14:1 WEB

I will not leave you orphans. I will come to you.

John 14:18 NHEB

Teaching them to observe all things that I commanded you. Behold, I am with you always, even to the end of the age.

Matthew 28:20 NHEB

Be free from the love of money, content with such things as you have, for he has said, "I will never leave you or forsake you."

Hebrews 13:5 NHEB

Beloved, do not be astonished at the fiery trial which has come upon you, to test you, as though a strange thing happened to you. But because you are partakers of Christ's sufferings, rejoice; that at the revelation of his glory you also may rejoice with exceeding joy.

1 Peter 4:12-13 NHEB

Humble yourselves therefore under the mighty hand of God, that he may exalt you in due time; casting all your worries on him, because he cares for you.

1 Peter 5:6-7 WEB

He also spoke a parable to them that they must always pray, and not give up.

Luke 18:1 WEB

Blessed be the God and Father of our Lord Jesus Christ, the Father of mercies and God of all comfort; who comforts us in all our affliction, that we may be able to comfort those who are in any affliction, through the comfort with which we ourselves are comforted by God.

2 Corinthians 1:3-4 NHEB

I will not leave you orphans. I will come to you.

John 14:18 NHEB

I will be to you a Father. You will be to me sons and daughters, says the Lord Almighty.

2 Corinthians 6:18 NHEB

And in him you are made full, who is the head of all principality and power.

Colossians 2:10 WEB

Why are you in despair, my soul? Why are you disturbed within me? Hope in God! For I shall still praise him for the saving help of his presence.

Psalm 42:5 NHEB

NOTES

When I get Angry

In any controversy the instant we feel anger
we have already ceased striving for truth,
and have begun striving for ourselves.

ANONYMOUS

❖

So, then, my beloved brothers, let every man be swift to hear, slow to speak, and slow to anger; for the anger of man doesn't produce the righteousness of God.

James 1:19-20 WEB

Be subject therefore to God. But resist the devil, and he will flee from you. Draw near to God, and he will draw near to you. Cleanse your hands, you sinners; and purify your hearts, you double-minded.

James 4:7-8 WEB

But I tell you, that everyone who is angry with his brother shall be in danger of the judgment; and whoever shall say to his brother, 'You good-for-nothing!' shall be in danger of the council; and whoever shall say, 'You fool!' shall be in danger of the fire of hell. "If therefore you are offering your gift at the altar, and there remember that your brother has anything against you, leave your gift there before the altar, and go your way. First be reconciled to your brother, and then come and offer your gift.

Matthew 5:22-24 NHEB

"For if you forgive men their trespasses, your heavenly Father will also forgive you."

Matthew 6:14 NHEB

"Be angry, and don't sin." Don't let the sun go down on your wrath.

Ephesians 4:26 WEB

Let all bitterness, wrath, anger, outcry, and slander, be put away from you, with all malice. And be kind to one another, tender hearted, forgiving each other, just as God also in Christ forgave you.

Ephesians 4:31-32 WEB

Don't seek revenge yourselves, beloved, but give place to God's wrath. For it is written, "Vengeance belongs to me; I will repay, says the Lord".

Romans 12:19 WEB

For you died, and your life is hidden with Christ in God.

Colossians 3:3 NHEB

For we know him who said, "Vengeance belongs to me; I will repay." Again, "The Lord will judge his people."

Hebrews 10:30 NHEB

Fathers, do not provoke your children, so that they won't be discouraged.

Colossians 3:21 NHEB

But I say to you, that whoever is angry with his brother without a cause shall be in danger of the judgment: and whoever shall say to his brother, 'Raca', shall be in danger of the council: but whoever shall say, You fool!, shall be in danger of hell fire.

Matthew 5:22 AKJV

For his anger endures but a moment; in his favor is life: weeping may endure for a night, but joy comes in the morning

Psalm 30:5 AKJV

Cease from anger, and forsake wrath. Don't fret, it leads only to evildoing.

Psalm 37:8 WEB

Therefore, put on the whole armor of God, that you may be able to withstand in the evil day, and, having done all, to stand.

Ephesians 6:13 NHEB

Be sober and self-controlled. Be watchful. Your adversary the devil, walks around like a roaring lion, seeking whom he may devour. Withstand him steadfast in your faith, knowing that your brothers who are in the world are undergoing the same sufferings.

1 Peter 5:8-9 NHEB

Yahweh is gracious, merciful, slow to anger, and of great loving kindness.

Psalm 145:8 WEB

He who is quick to become angry will commit folly, and a crafty man is hated.

Proverbs 14:17 NHEB

A wrathful man stirs up contention, but one who is slow to anger appeases strife.

Proverbs 15:18 NHEB

For in as much as he himself has suffered and has been tempted, he also is able to assist those who are tempted.

Hebrews 2:18 CPDV

You are of God, little children, and have overcome them; because greater is he who is in you than he who is in the world.

1 John 4:4 NHEB

Let no man say when he is tempted, "I am tempted by God," for God cannot be tempted by evil, and he himself tempts no one. But each one is tempted, when he is drawn away by his own lust, and enticed.

James 1:13-14 NHEB

This you know, my beloved brothers. But let every man be swift to hear, slow to speak, and slow to anger.

James 1:19 NHEB

One who is slow to anger is better than the mighty; one who rules his spirit, than he who takes a city.

Proverbs 16:32 NHEB

The discretion of a man makes him slow to anger. It is his glory to overlook an offense.

Proverbs 19:11 WEB

It is better to dwell in a desert land, than with a contentious and fretful woman.

Proverbs 21:19 WEB

Don't befriend a hot-tempered man, and don't associate with one who harbors anger: lest you learn his ways.

Proverbs 22:24-25 WEB

If your enemy is hungry, give him food to eat. If he is thirsty, give him water to drink: for you will heap coals of fire on his head, and Yahweh will reward you.

Proverbs 25:21-22 WEB

A stone is heavy, and sand is a burden; but a fool's provocation is heavier than both.

Proverb 27:3 NHEB

Wrath is cruel, and anger is overwhelming; but who is able to stand before jealousy?

Proverbs 27:4 WEB

He who blesses his neighbor with a loud voice early in the morning, it will be taken as a curse by him.

Proverbs 27:14 NHEB

An angry man stirs up strife, and a wrathful man abounds in sin.

Proverbs 29:22 WEB

He who is slow to anger has great understanding, but he who has a quick temper displays folly.

Proverbs 14:29 NHEB

A gentle answer turns away wrath, but a harsh word stirs up anger.

Proverbs 15:1 NHEB

The north wind brings forth rain: so a backbiting tongue brings an angry face.

Proverbs 25:23 NHEB

A wise man fears, and shuns evil, but the fool is hotheaded and reckless.

Proverbs 14:16 NHEB

NOTES

In Him I have Strength and Security

✤

My sheep hear my voice, and I know them, and they follow me. I give eternal life to them. They will never perish, and no one will snatch them out of my hand. My Father, who has given them to me, is greater than all. No one is able to snatch them out of the Father's hand.

John 10:27-29 NHEB

"Do not work for the food which perishes, but for the food which remains to eternal life, which the Son of Man will give to you. For God the Father has sealed him."

John 6:27 NHEB

All those whom the Father gives me will come to me. Him who comes to me I will in no way throw out.

John 6:37 NHEB

I can do all things through Christ which strengthens me.

Philippians 4:13 AKJV

Being confident of this very thing, that he which has begun a good work in you will perform it until the day of Jesus Christ.

Philippians 1:6 AKJV

Blessed be the God and Father of our Lord Jesus Christ, who has blessed us with every spiritual blessing in the heavenly places in Christ.

Ephesians 1:13 WEB

For this cause, I bow my knees before the Father, from whom every family in heaven and on earth is named, that he would grant you, according to the riches of his glory, that you may be strengthened with power through his Spirit in the inward man; that Christ may dwell in your hearts through faith; to the end that you, being rooted and grounded in love, may be strengthened to comprehend with all the saints what is the breadth and length and height and depth, and to know Christ's love which surpasses knowledge, that you may be filled with all the fullness of God. Now to him who is able to do exceedingly abundantly above all that we ask or think, according to the power that works in us.

Ephesians 3:14-20 NHEB

Do not grieve the Holy Spirit of God, in whom you were sealed for the day of redemption.

Ephesians 4:30 NHEB

Therefore, put on the whole armor of God, that you may be able to withstand in the evil day, and, having done all, to stand.

Ephesians 6:13 NHEB

For I am persuaded that neither death, nor life, nor angels, nor principalities, nor things present, nor things to come, nor powers, nor height, nor depth, nor any other created thing, will be able to separate us from God's love, which is in Christ Jesus our Lord.

Romans 8:38-39 WEB

Finally, be strong in the Lord, and in the strength of his might.

Ephesians 6:10 NHEB

Blessed be the God and Father of our Lord Jesus Christ, who according to his great mercy became our father again to a living hope through the resurrection of Jesus Christ from the dead, to an incorruptible and undefiled inheritance that does not fade away, reserved in Heaven for you, who by the power of God are guarded through faith for a salvation ready to be revealed in the last time. Wherein you greatly rejoice, though now for a little while, if necessary, you have been grieved by various trials.

1Peter 1:3-6 NHEB

But the Lord is faithful, who will establish you, and guard you from the evil one.

2 Thessalonians 3:3 WEB

Now he who establishes us with you in Christ, and anointed us, is God; who also sealed us, and gave us the down payment of the Spirit in our hearts.

2 Corinthians 1:21-22 NHEB

NOTES

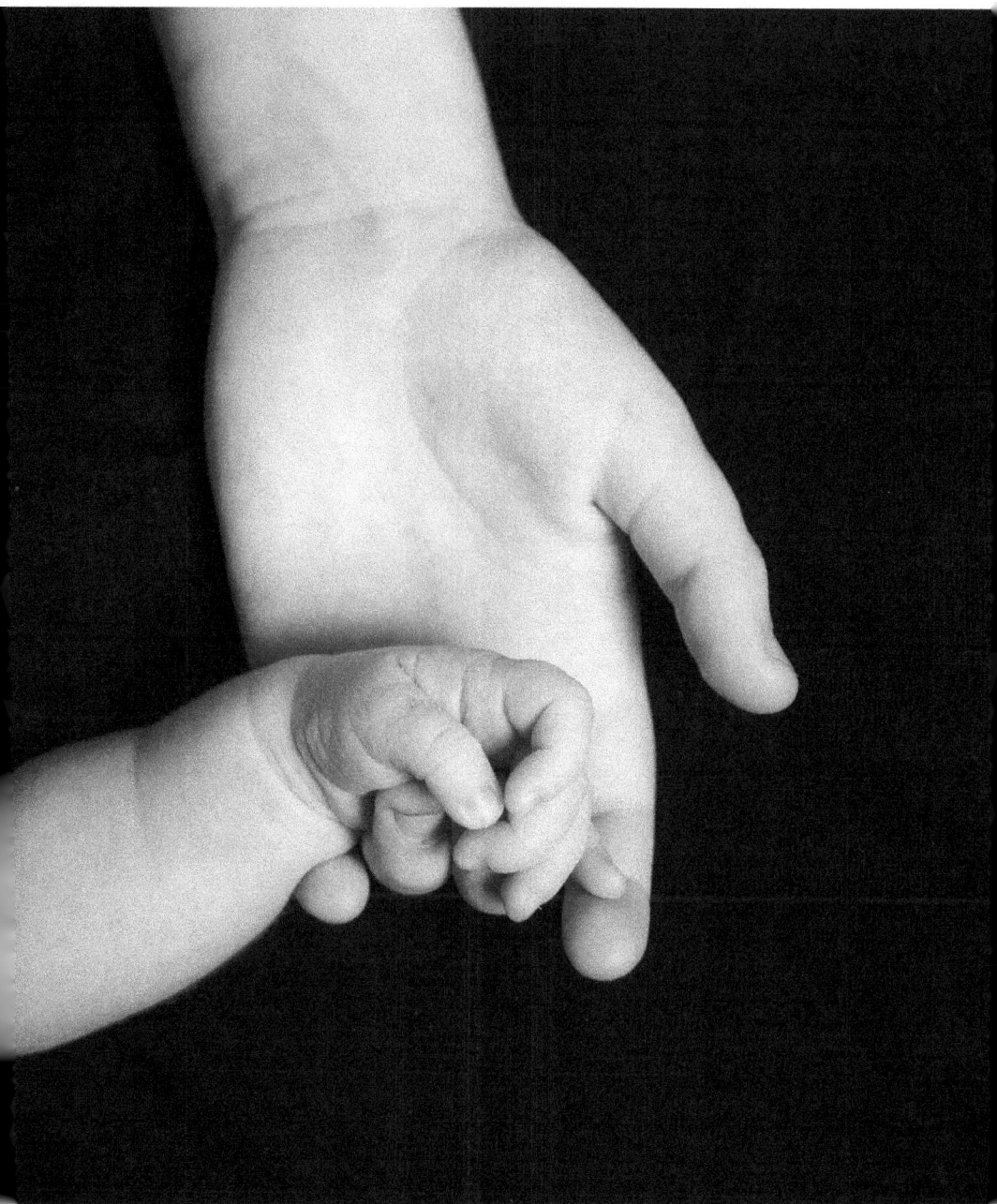

When I am Tempted

❖

For sin shall not have dominion over you: for you are not under the law, but under grace.

Romans 6:14 AKJV

Dearly beloved, avenge not yourselves, but rather give place to wrath: for it is written, Vengeance is mine; I will repay, said the Lord.

Romans 12:19 AKJV

Now the Lord is the Spirit and where the Spirit of the Lord is, there is liberty.

2 Corinthians 3:17 NHEB

Therefore, put on the whole armor of God, that you may be able to withstand in the evil day, and, having done all, to stand.

Ephesians 6:13 NHEB

Be sober and self-controlled. Be watchful. Your adversary, the devil, walks around like a roaring lion, seeking whom he may devour. Withstand him steadfast in your faith, knowing that your brothers who are in the world are undergoing the same sufferings.

1 Peter 5:8-9 WEB

Be subject therefore to God. But resist the devil, and he will flee from you.

James 4:7 WEB

Count it all joy, my brothers, when you fall into various temptations, knowing that the testing of your faith produces endurance.

James 1:2-3 WEB

Wherein you greatly rejoice, though now for a little while, if necessary, you have been grieved by various trials. that the genuineness of your faith, which is more precious than gold that perishes even though it is tested by fire, may be found to result in praise, glory, and honor at the revelation of Jesus Christ.

1 Peter 1: 6-7 NHEB

But if any of you lacks wisdom, let him ask of God, who gives to all liberally and without reproach; and it will be given to him.

James 1:5 WEB

Blessed is the man who endures temptation, for when he has been approved, he will receive the crown of life, which the Lord promised to those who love him. Let no man say when he is tempted, "I am tempted by God," for God can't be tempted by evil, and he himself tempts no one. But each one is tempted when he is drawn away by his own lust, and enticed.

James 1:12-14 WEB

For we know him who said, "Vengeance belongs to me," says the Lord, "I will repay. Again, "The Lord will judge his people."

Hebrews 10:30 WEB

Finally, be strong in the Lord, and in the strength of his might. Put on the whole armor of God that you may be able to stand against the wiles of the devil. Above all, taking up the shield of faith, with which you will be able to quench all the fiery darts of the evil one. And take the helmet of salvation, and the sword of the Spirit, which is the spoken word of God.

Ephesians 6:10-11, 16-17 NHEB

No temptation has taken you except what is common to man. God is faithful, who will not allow you to be tempted above what you are able, but will with the temptation also make the way of escape, that you may be able to endure it.

1 Corinthians 10-13 WEB

NOTES

No room for Fear when I have Faith

*So many are loaded down with "religion" instead
of being lifted by true faith that sustains.*

V A Hays

⚜

And when he had arrived at the house, the blind men approached him. And Jesus said to them, "Do you trust that I am able to do this for you?" They say to him, "Certainly, Lord.

Matthew 9:28 CPDV

So he said to them, "Because of your little faith. For truly I tell you, if you have faith as a grain of mustard seed, you will tell this mountain, 'Move from here to there,' and it will move; and nothing will be impossible for you."

Matthew 17:20 NHEB

For as many as are led by the Spirit of God, these are children of God. For you did not receive the spirit of bondage again to fear, but you received the Spirit of adoption, by whom we cry, "Abba! Father!"

Romans 8:14-15 NHEB

I have fought the good fight. I have finished the course. I have kept the faith.

2 Timothy 4:7 NHEB

Without faith it is impossible to be well pleasing to him, for he who comes to God must believe that he exists, and that he is a rewarder of those who seek him.

Hebrews 11:6 WEB

Looking to Jesus, the author and finisher of our faith, who for the joy that was set before him endured the cross, disregarding its shame, and has sat down at the right hand of the throne of God.

Hebrews 12:2 NHEB

For I say, through the grace that was given me, to every man who is among you, not to think of himself more highly than he ought to think; but to think reasonably, as God has apportioned to each person a measure of faith.

Romans 12-3 WEB

For in it is revealed God's righteousness from faith to faith. As it is written, "But the righteous shall live by faith."

Romans 1:17 NHEB

Behold, a woman who had an issue of blood for twelve years came behind him, and touched the fringe of his garment; for she said within herself, "If I just touch his garment, I will be made well." But Jesus, turning around and seeing her, said, "Daughter, cheer up! Your faith has made you well." And the woman was made well from that hour.

Matthew 9:20-22 WEB

Therefore, faith is from hearing, and hearing is through the Word of Christ.

Romans 10:17 CPDV

That the genuineness of your faith, which is more precious than gold that perishes even though it is tested by fire, may be found to result in praise, glory, and honor at the revelation of Jesus Christ—whom not having seen you love; in whom, though now you do not see him, yet believing, you rejoice greatly with joy inexpressible and full of glory—receiving the result of your faith, the salvation of your souls.

1 Peter 1:7-9 NHEB

Peace I leave with you. My peace I give to you. I do not give to you as the world gives. Do not let your heart be troubled, neither let it be afraid.

John 14:27 NHEB

For we walk by faith, not by sight.

2 Corinthians 5:7 WEB

So that with good courage we say, "The Lord is my helper. I will not fear. What can man do to me?"

Hebrews 13:6 NHEB

Now faith is assurance of things hoped for, proof of things not seen.

Hebrews 11:1 WEB

For whatever is born of God overcomes the world. This is the victory that has overcome the world: your faith.

1 John 5:4 WEB

And the prayer of faith will heal him who is sick, and the Lord will raise him up. If he has committed sins, he will be forgiven.

James 5:15 WEB

Jesus said to him, "If you can believe, all things are possible to him who believes."

Mark 9:23 WEB

Do not be afraid, little flock; for it has pleased your Father to give you the kingdom.

Luke 12:32 CPDV

Don't be afraid of those who kill the body, but are not able to kill the soul. Rather, fear him who is able to destroy both soul and body in Gehenna.

Matthew 10:28 WEB

For God didn't give us a spirit of fear, but of power, love, and self-control.

2 Timothy 1:7 WEB

For the eyes of the Lord are on the righteous, and his ears open to their prayer; but the face of the Lord is against those who do evil." Now who is he who will harm you, if you become zealous of that which is good? But even if you should suffer for righteousness' sake, you are blessed. "Do not fear what they fear, neither be troubled."

1 Peter 3:12-14 NHEB

Even though I walk through the valley of the shadow of death, I will fear no evil, for you are with me. Your rod and your staff, they comfort me. You prepare a table before me in the presence of my enemies. You anoint my head with oil. My cup runs over.

Psalms 23:4-5 NHEB

For in the day of trouble he will keep me secretly in his pavilion. In the covert of his tabernacle he will hide me. He will lift me up on a rock.

Psalm 27:5 NHEB

God is our refuge and strength, a very present help in trouble.

Psalm 46:1 NHEB

He will cover you with his feathers. Under his wings you will take refuge. His faithfulness is your shield and rampart. You shall not be afraid of the terror by night, nor of the arrow that flies by day; nor of the pestilence that walks in darkness, nor of the destruction that wastes at noonday.

Psalm 91:4-6 NHEB

But whoever listens to me will dwell securely, and will be at ease, without fear of harm.

Proverb 1:33 NHEB

When you lie down, you will not be afraid. Yes, you will lie down, and your sleep will be sweet. Do not be afraid of sudden fear or of the storm of the wicked when it comes: for the LORD will be your confidence, and will keep your foot from being taken.

Proverb 3:24-26 NHEB

The fear of man proves to be a snare, but whoever puts his trust in the LORD is kept safe.

Proverb 29:25 NHEB

NOTES

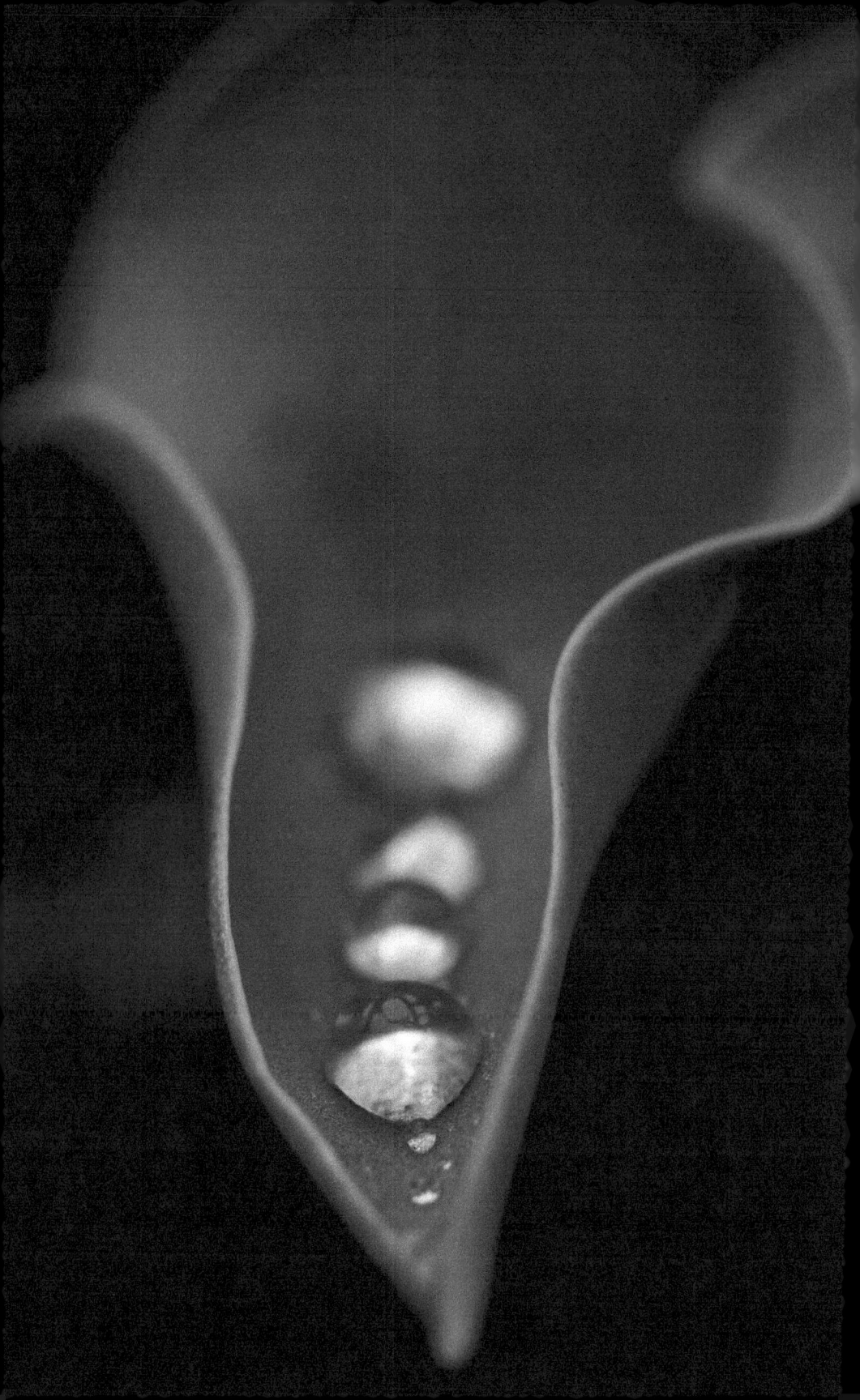

I can have Courage and Confidence

There is only a slight difference between keeping your chin up and sticking your neck out, but it's worth knowing.

ANONYMOUS

✤

In nothing be anxious, but in everything, by prayer and petition with thanksgiving, let your requests be made known to God.

Philippians 4:6 WEB

I can do all things through Christ, who strengthens me.

Philippians 4:13 WEB

Therefore do not throw away your boldness, which has a great reward. For you need patient endurance so that, having done the will of God, you may receive the promise.

Hebrews 10:35-36 NHEB

And the peace of God, which surpasses all understanding, will guard your hearts and your thoughts in Christ Jesus. Finally, brothers, whatever things are true, whatever things are honorable, whatever things are just, whatever things are pure, whatever things are lovely, whatever things are of good report; if there is any virtue, and if there is any praise, think about these things.

Philippians 4:7-8 WEB

Beloved, if our hearts do not condemn us, we have boldness toward God.

1 John 3:21 NHEB

This is the boldness which we have toward him, that, if we ask anything according to his will, he listens to us. And if we know that he listens to us, whatever we ask, we know that we have the petitions which we have asked of him.

1 John 5:14-15 NHEB

Beloved, do not be astonished at the fiery trial which has come upon you, to test you, as though a strange thing happened to you. But because you are partakers of Christ's sufferings, rejoice; that at the revelation of his glory you also may rejoice with exceeding joy.

1 Peter 4:12-13 NHEB

So that with good courage we say, "The Lord is my helper. I will not fear. What can man do to me?"

Hebrews 13:6 NHEB

Being confident of this very thing, that he who began a good work in you will complete it until the day of Jesus Christ.

Philippians 1:6 WEB

Most certainly I tell you, he who believes in me, the works that I do, he will do also; and he will do greater works than these, because I am going to my Father. Whatever you will ask in my name, that will I do, that the Father may be glorified in the Son. If you will ask anything in my name, I will do it.

John 14:12-14 WEB

No, in all these things, we are more than conquerors through him who loved us.

Romans 8:37 WEB

I rejoice that in everything I am confident concerning you.

2 Corinthians 7:16 WEB

I have fought the good fight. I have finished the course. I have kept the faith.

2 Timothy 4:7 WEB

Wait for the LORD. Be strong, and let your heart take courage. Yes, wait for the LORD.

Psalm 27:14 NHEB

Be strong, and let your heart take courage, all you who hope in the LORD.

Psalm 31:24 NHEB

Trust in the LORD, and do good. Dwell in the land, and enjoy safe pasture.

Psalm 37:3 NHEB

For the LORD loves justice, and doesn't forsake his holy ones. They are preserved forever, but the children of the wicked shall be cut off. The righteous shall inherit the land, and live in it forever.

Psalm 37:38-39 NHEB

And the God of peace will quickly crush Satan under your feet. The grace of our Lord Jesus Christ be with you.

Romans 16:20 WEB

Therefore, prepare your minds for action, be sober and set your hope fully on the grace that will be brought to you at the revelation of Jesus Christ.

1 Peter 1:13 NHEB

For I am persuaded, that neither death, nor life, nor angels, nor principalities, nor things present, nor things to come, nor powers, nor height, nor depth, nor any other created thing, will be able to separate us from the love of God, which is I Christ Jesus our Lord.

Romans 8:38-39 NHEB

In whom we have boldness and access in confidence through our faith in him.

Ephesians 3:12 NHEB

Watch! Stand firm in the faith! Be courageous! Be strong!

1 Corinthians 16:13 WEB

NOTES

He gives Comfort in Sickness and Sorrow

Love your own soul, and comfort your heart,
remove sorrow from you: for sorrow has killed
many, and there is not profit therein.

ANONYMOUS

❖

Blessed be the God and Father of our Lord Jesus Christ, the Father of mercies and God of all comfort; who comforts us in all our affliction, that we may be able to comfort those who are in any affliction, through the comfort with which we ourselves are comforted by God.

2 Corinthians 1:3-4 WEB

We are courageous, I say, and are willing rather to be absent from the body, and to be at home with the Lord.

2 Corinthians 5:8 WEB

Beloved, I pray that you may prosper in all things and be healthy, even as your soul prospers.

3 John 2 WEB

Cast all your worries on him, because he cares for you.

1 Peter 5:7 WEB

Who his own self bore our sins in his body on the tree, that we, having died to sins, might live to righteousness; by his stripes you were healed.

1 Peter 2:24 NHEB

And responding, the centurion said: "Lord, I am not worthy that you should enter under my roof, but only say the word, and my servant shall be healed.

Matthew 8:8 CPDV

Is any among you sick? Let him call for the elders of the church, and let them pray over him, anointing him with oil in the name of the Lord, and the prayer of faith will heal him who is sick, and the Lord will raise him up. If he has committed sins, he will be forgiven. Therefore confess your sins to one another, and pray for one another, that you may be healed. The insistent prayer of the righteous is powerfully effective.

James 5:14-16 NHEB

Until I come, pay attention to reading, to exhortation, and to teaching. Do not neglect the gift that is in you, which was given to you by prophecy, with the laying on of the hands of the elders.

1 Timothy 4:13-14 NHEB

Now our Lord Jesus Christ himself, and God our Father, who loved us and gave us eternal comfort and good hope through grace, comfort your hearts and establish you in every good work and word.

2 Thessalonians 2:16-17 WEB

"Death, where is your sting? Hades, where is your victory?" The sting of death is sin, and the power of sin is the law. But thanks be to God, who gives us the victory through our Lord Jesus Christ.

1 Corinthians 15:55-57 WEB

He will wipe away from them every tear from their eyes. Death will be no more; neither will there be mourning, nor crying, nor pain, any more. The first things have passed away."

Revelation 21:4 WEB

Let us therefore draw near with boldness to the throne of grace, that we may receive mercy, and may find grace for help in time of need.

Hebrews 4:16 NHEB

In the same way, the Spirit also helps our weaknesses, for we don't know how to pray as we ought. But the Spirit himself makes intercession for us with groanings which can't be uttered. He who searches the hearts knows what is on the Spirit's mind, because he makes intercession for the saints according to God.

Romans 8:26-27 WEB

Therefore, you also, indeed, have sorrow now. But I will see you again, and your heart shall rejoice. And no one will take away your joy from you.

John 16:22 CPDV

Jesus went about in all Galilee, teaching in their synagogues, preaching the Good News of the Kingdom, and healing every disease and every sickness among the people. The report about him went out into all Syria. They brought to him all who were sick, afflicted with various diseases and torments, possessed with demons, epileptics, and paralytics; and he healed them.

Matthew 4:23-24 WEB

But that you may know that the Son of Man has authority on earth to forgive sins..." (Then he said to the paralytic), "Get up, and take up your mat, and go up to your house." And he arose and departed to his house.

Matthew 9:6-7 NHEB

For the needy shall not always be forgotten, nor the hope of the poor perish forever.

Psalm 9:18 NHEB

Hope deferred makes the heart sick, but when longing is fulfilled, it is a tree of life.

Proverb 13:12 NHEB

And the prayer of faith will heal him who is sick, and the Lord will raise him up. If he has committed sins, he will be forgiven.

James 5:15 WEB

NOTES

He gives me time for Patience

Adopt the pace of nature: her secret is patience.

RALPH WALDO EMERSON

♦

Count it all joy, my brothers, when you fall into various temptations, knowing that the testing of your faith produces endurance. Let endurance have its perfect work, that you may be perfect and complete, lacking in nothing.

James 1:2-4 WEB

Be patient therefore, brothers, until the coming of the Lord. Behold, the farmer waits for the precious fruit of the earth, being patient over it, until it receives the early and late rain. You also be patient. Establish your hearts, for the coming of the Lord is near.

James 5:7-8 NHEB

But the fruit of the Spirit is love, joy, peace, patience, kindness, goodness, faithfulness, gentleness, and self-control. Against such things there is no law.

Galatians 5:22-23 NHEB

Not only this, but we also rejoice in our sufferings, knowing that suffering produces perseverance; and perseverance, proven character; and proven character, hope: and hope doesn't disappoint us, because God's love has been poured out into our hearts through the Holy Spirit who was given to us.

Romans 5:3-5 WEB

But if we hope for that which we don't see, we wait for it with patience.

Romans 8:25 NHEB

That you be not slothful, but followers of them who through faith and patience inherit the promises.

Hebrews 6:12 AKJV

For whatever things were written before were written for our learning, that through patience and through encouragement of the Scriptures we might have hope. Now the God of patience and of encouragement grant you to be of the same mind one with another according to Christ Jesus.

Romans 15:4-5 NHEB

Therefore do not throw away your boldness, which has a great reward. For you need patient endurance so that, having done the will of God, you may receive the promise. "In a very little while, he who comes will come, and will not wait.

Hebrews 10:35-37 AKJV

Therefore let us also, seeing we are surrounded by so great a cloud of witnesses, lay aside every weight and the sin which so easily entangles us, and let us run with patience the race that is set before us.

Hebrews 12:1 NHEB

For what glory is it if, when you sin, you patiently endure beating? But if, when you do well, you patiently endure suffering, this is commendable with God.

1 Peter 2:20 NHEB

Let us hold fast the confession of our hope without wavering; for he who promised is faithful.

Hebrews 10:23 NHEB

Wait on the LORD: be of good courage, and he shall strengthen your heart: wait, I say, on the LORD.

Psalm 27:14 AKJV

NOTES

He covers me with Peace

*If I am at war with myself, I can bring
little peace to my fellow man.*

ANONYMOUS

✦

But now in Christ Jesus you who once were far off are made near in the blood of Christ. For he is our peace, who made both one, and broke down the middle wall of partition.

Ephesians 2:13-14 NHEB

In nothing be anxious, but in everything, by prayer and petition with thanksgiving, let your requests be made known to God. And the peace of God, which surpasses all understanding, will guard your hearts and your thoughts in Christ Jesus.

Philippians 4:6-7 WEB

Now may the Lord of peace himself give you peace at all times in all ways. The Lord be with you all.

2 Thessalonians 3:16 WEB

For God's Kingdom is not eating and drinking, but righteousness, peace, and joy in the Holy Spirit. For he who serves Christ in these things is acceptable to God and approved by men. So then, let us follow after things which make for peace, and things by which we may build one another up.

Romans 14:17-19 WEB

Finally, brothers, rejoice. Be perfected, be comforted, be of the same mind, live in peace, and the God of love and peace will be with you.

2 Corinthians 13:11 WEB

The things which you learned, received, heard, and saw in me: do these things, and the God of peace will be with you.

Philippians 4:9 WEB

And let the peace of God rule in your hearts, to which also you were called in one body; and be thankful.

Colossians 3:15 WEB

Being therefore justified by faith, we have peace with God through our Lord Jesus Christ.

Romans 5:1 WEB

And the God of peace will quickly crush Satan under your feet. The grace of our Lord Jesus Christ be with you.

Romans 16:20 WEB

Peace I leave for you; my Peace I give to you. Not in the way that the world gives, do I give to you. Do not let your heart be troubled, and let it not fear. You have heard that I said to you: I am going away, and I am returning to you. If you loved me, certainly you would be gladdened, because I am going to the Father. For the Father is greater than I.

John 14:27-28 CPDV

And he said to the woman, your faith has saved you; go in peace.

Luke 7:50 AKJV

And let the peace of Christ rule in your hearts, to which also you were called in one body; and be thankful.

Colossians 3:15 NHEB

Therefore, prepare your minds for action, be sober and set your hope fully on the grace that will be brought to you at the revelation of Jesus Christ.

1 Peter 1:13 NHEB

The LORD will give strength to his people; the LORD will bless his people with peace.

Psalm 29:11 AKJV

But the meek shall inherit the earth; and shall delight themselves in the abundance of peace.

Psalm 37:11 AKJV

For the mind of the flesh is death, but the mind of the Spirit is life and peace.

Romans 8:6 NHEB

Now may the God of hope fill you with all joy and peace in believing, that you may abound in hope, in the power of the Holy Spirit.

Romans 15:13 NHEB

Blessed are the peacemakers, for they shall be called sons of God.

Matthew 5:9 CPDV

Mark the perfect man, and see the upright, for there is a future for the man of peace.

Psalm 37:37 NHEB

I will hear what God, the LORD, will speak, for he will speak peace to his people, his holy ones; but let them not turn again to folly.

Psalm 85:8 NHEB

Mercy and truth meet together. Righteousness and peace have kissed each other.

Psalm 85:10 NHEB

Her ways are ways of pleasantness. All her paths are peace.

Proverbs 3:17 NHEB

Deceit is in the heart of those who plot evil, but joy comes to the promoters of peace.

Proverbs 12:20 NHEB

When a man's ways please the LORD, he makes even his enemies to be at peace with him.

Proverbs 16:7 NHEB

NOTES

I can stand in Authority
and Obedience

Sin is not harmful because it is forbidden,
but it is forbidden because it is harmful.

BENJAMIN FRANKLIN

For the Kingdom of God is not eating and drinking, but righteousness, peace, and joy in the Holy Spirit. For he who serves Christ in these things is acceptable to God and approved by men. So then, let us follow after things which make for peace, and things by which we may build one another.

Romans 14:17-19 NHEB

Knowing this first, that no prophecy of Scripture is of private interpretation. For no prophecy ever came by the will of man: but holy men of God spoke, being moved by the Holy Spirit.

2 Peter 1:20-21 WEB

For however many are the promises of God, in him is the "Yes." Therefore through him is the "Amen", to the glory of God through us.

2 Corinthians 1:20 WEB

But Peter and the apostles answered, "We must obey God rather than men.

Acts 5:29 NHEB

Every Scripture is God-breathed and profitable for teaching, for reproof, for correction, and for instruction in righteousness, that the man of God may be complete, thoroughly equipped for every good work.

2 Timothy 3:16-17 WEB

This is how we know that we know him: if we keep his commandments. One who says, "I know him," and doesn't keep his commandments, is a liar, and the truth isn't in him. But whoever keeps his word, God's love has most certainly been perfected in him. This is how we know that we are in him: he who says he remains in him ought himself also to walk just like he walked.

1 John 2:3-6 WEB

For the word of God is living, and active, and sharper than any two-edged sword, and piercing even to the dividing of soul and spirit, of both joints and marrow, and is able to discern the thoughts and intentions of the heart.

Hebrews 4:12 NHEB

"You search the Scriptures, because you think that in them you have eternal life; and these are they which testify about me."

John 5:39 NHEB

Seeing you have purified your souls in your obedience to the truth in sincere brotherly affection, love one another from a pure heart fervently: having been born again, not of corruptible seed, but of incorruptible, through the living and abiding Word of God. For, "All flesh is like grass, and all its glory like the flower in the grass. The grass withers, and its flower falls; but the word of the Lord endures forever." This is the word of Good News which was preached to you.

1 Peter 1:22-25 NHEB

Heaven and earth shall pass away, but my word shall not pass away.

Mark 13:31 CPDV

Subject yourselves to every ordinance of man for the Lord's sake: whether to the king, as supreme; or to governors, as sent by him for vengeance on evildoers and for praise to those who do well. For this is the will of God, that by well-doing you should put to silence the ignorance of foolish men: as free, and not using your freedom for a cloak of wickedness, but as bondservants of God. Honor all men. Love the brotherhood. Fear God. Honor the king. Servants, be in subjection to your masters with all fear; not only to the good and gentle, but also to the wicked. For it is commendable if someone endures pain, suffering unjustly, because of conscience toward God. For what glory is it if, when you sin, you patiently endure beating? But if, when you do well, you patiently endure suffering, this is commendable with God.

1 Peter 2 13:-20 NHEB

Children, obey your parents in the Lord, for this is right. "Honor your father and mother," which is the first commandment with a promise: "that it may be well with you, and you may live long on the earth." And fathers, do not provoke your children to anger, but nurture them in the discipline and instruction of the Lord.

Ephesians 6:1-4 NHEB

If you love me, keep my commandments. Whoever holds to my commandments and keeps them: it is he who loves me. And whoever loves me shall be loved by my Father. And I will love him, and I will manifest myself to him."

John 14:15, 21 CPDV

Whoever therefore shall break one of these least commandments, and shall teach men so, he shall be called the least in the kingdom of heaven: but whoever shall do and teach them, the same shall be called great in the kingdom of heaven.

Matthew 5:19 KJV

Not everyone who says to me, 'Lord, Lord,' will enter into the Kingdom of Heaven; but he who does the will of my Father who is in heaven. "Everyone therefore who hears these words of mine, and does them, will be compared to a wise man, who built his house on a rock. And the rain came down, the floods came, and the winds blew, and beat on that house; and it did not fall, for it was founded on the rock.

Matthew 7:21, 24-25 NHEB

Jesus responded and said to him: "If anyone loves me, he shall keep my word. And my Father will love him, and we will come to him, and we will make our dwelling place with him.

John 14:23 CPDV

If you know these things, happy are you if you do them.

John 13:17 AKJV

If you keep my commandments, you shall abide in my love; even as I have kept my Father's commandments, and abide in his love.

John 15:10 AKJV

Amen, amen, I say to you, that whoever hears my word, and believes in him who sent me, has eternal life, and he does not go into judgment, but instead he crosses from death into life.

John 5:24 CPDV

But he who looks into the perfect Law of freedom, and continues, not being a hearer who forgets, but a doer of the work, this man will be blessed in what he does.

James 1:25 NHEB

For it is not the hearers of the law who are righteous before God, but the doers of the law will be justified.

Romans 2:13 NHEB

"For anyone who does the will of my Father, who is in heaven, the same is my brother, and sister, and mother."

Matthew 12:50 NHEB

The world is passing away with its lusts, but he who does God's will remains forever.

1 John 2:17 WEB

And whatever we ask, we receive from him, because we keep his commandments and do the things that are pleasing in his sight.

1 John 3:22 NHEB

If you love me, keep my commandments.

John 14:15 AKJV

For the LORD God is a sun and a shield. The LORD will give grace and glory. He withholds no good thing from those who walk blamelessly.

Psalm 84:11 NHEB

As an earring of gold, and an ornament of fine gold, so is a wise reprover to an obedient ear.

Proverbs 25:12 WEB

"The eye that mocks at his father, and scorns obedience to his mother: the ravens of the valley shall pick it out; the young eagles shall eat it.

Proverbs 30:17 WEB

NOTES

Money, Money Everywhere

A visa may get you to the Golden
Gate, but never to Heaven's.

V A Hays

❖

"Give, and it will be given to you: good measure, pressed down, shaken together, and running over, will be given to you. For with the same measure you measure it will be measured back to you."

Luke 6:38 AKJV

But if this is how God clothes the grass in the field, which today exists, and tomorrow is cast into the oven, how much more will he clothe you, O you of little faith? Do not seek what you will eat or what you will drink; neither be anxious. For the nations of the world seek after all of these things, but your Father knows that you need these things.

Luke 12:28 NHEB

Be free from the love of money, content with such things as you have, for he has said, "I will never leave you or forsake you."

Hebrews 13:5 NHEB

Beloved, I pray that you may prosper in all things and be healthy, even as your soul prospers.

3 John 2 AKJV

Do not choose to store up for yourselves treasures on earth: where rust and moth consume, and where thieves break in and steal. Instead, store up for yourselves treasures in heaven: where neither rust nor moth consumes, and where thieves do not break in and steal. For where your treasure is, there also is your heart.

Matthew 6:19-21 CPDV

Therefore, do not choose to be anxious, saying: 'What shall we eat, and what shall we drink, and with what shall we be clothed? For the Gentiles seek all these things. Yet your Father knows that you need all these things. Therefore, seek first the kingdom of God and his justice, and all these things shall be added to you as well.

Matthew 6:31-33 CPDV

Now concerning the collection for the saints, as I commanded the assemblies of Galatia, you do likewise. On the first day of the week, let each one of you save, as he may prosper, that no collections be made when I come.

1 Corinthians 16:1-2 WEB

Remember this: he who sows sparingly will also reap sparingly. He who sows bountifully will also reap bountifully. Let each man give according as he has determined in his heart; not grudgingly, or under compulsion; for God loves a cheerful giver. And God is able to make all grace abound to you, that you, always having all sufficiency in everything, may abound to every good work.

2 Corinthians 9:6-8 NHEB

My God will supply every need of yours according to his riches in glory in Christ Jesus.

Philippians 4:19 NHEB

Heal the sick, cleanse the lepers, and cast out demons. Freely you received, so freely give.

Matthew 10:8 WEB

Everyone who has left houses, or brothers, or sisters, or father, or mother, or wife, or children, or lands, for my name's sake, will receive one hundred times, and will inherit eternal life.

Matthew 19:29 WEB

For who has known the mind of the Lord? Or who has been his counselor? Or who has first given to him, and it will be repaid to him again? For of him, and through him, and to him, are all things. To him be the glory forever! Amen.

Romans 11:35-36 NHEB

And he sat down opposite the treasury, and saw how the multitude cast money into the treasury. Many who were rich cast in much. A poor widow came, and she cast in two small brass coins, which equal a quadrans coin. He called his disciples to himself, and said to them, "Truly I tell you, this poor widow gave more than all those who are giving into the treasury, for they all gave out of their abundance, but she, out of her poverty, gave all that she had to live on.

Mark 12:41-44 NHEB

Listen, my beloved brothers. Did not God choose those who are poor in this world to be rich in faith, and heirs of the Kingdom which he promised to those who love him?

James 2:5 NHEB

Charge those who are rich in this present world that they not be haughty, nor have their hope set on the uncertainty of riches, but on God, who richly provides us with everything to enjoy; that they do good, that they be rich in good works, that they be ready to distribute, willing to communicate; laying up in store for themselves a good foundation against the time to come, that they may lay hold of that which is truly life.

1 Timothy 6:17-19 NHEB

For we brought nothing into the world. For the love of money is a root of all kinds of evil. Some have been led astray from the faith in their greed, and have pierced themselves through with many sorrows. And we certainly can't carry anything out.

1 Timothy 6:7, 10 WEB

And said, 'Cornelius, your prayer is heard, and your gifts to the needy are remembered in the sight of God.

Acts 10:31 WEB

For the needy shall not always be forgotten, nor the hope of the poor perish forever.

Psalm 9:18 WEB

"Because of the oppression of the weak and because of the groaning of the needy, I will now arise," says the LORD; "I will set him in safety from those who malign him."

Psalm 12:5 NHEB

Better is a little that the righteous has, than the abundance of many wicked.

Psalm 37:16 NHEB

Happy is he who considers the poor. The LORD will deliver him in the day of evil.

Psalm 41:1 NHEB

Your congregation lived therein. You, God, prepared your goodness for the poor.

Psalm 68:10 NHEB

He has responded to the prayer of the destitute, and has not despised their prayer.

Psalm 102:17 NHEB

Riches do not profit in the day of wrath, but righteousness delivers from death.

Proverb 11:4 NHEB

He who trusts in his riches will fall, but the righteous shall flourish as the green leaf.

Proverb 11:28 NHEB

Wealth gained dishonestly dwindles away, but he who gathers by hand makes it grow.

Proverb 13:11 NHEB

Better is little, with the fear of the LORD, than great treasure with trouble.

Proverb 15:16 NHEB

Whoever mocks the poor reproaches his Maker. He who is glad at calamity shall not be unpunished.

Proverb 17:5 NHEB

The rich and the poor have this in common: The LORD is the maker of them all.

Proverb 22:2 NHEB

Whoever oppresses the poor for his own increase and whoever gives to the rich, both come to poverty.

Proverb 22:16 NHEB

Do not exploit the poor, because he is poor; and do not crush the needy in court.

Proverb 22:22 NHEB

Do not weary yourself to be rich. In your wisdom, show restraint. Why do you set your eyes on that which is not? For it certainly sprouts wings like an eagle and flies in the sky.

Proverb 23:4-5 NHEB

Better is the poor who walks in his integrity, than he who is perverse in his ways, and he is rich.

Proverb 28:6 NHEB

A faithful man is rich with blessings; but one who is eager to be rich will not go unpunished.

Proverb 28:20 NHEB

A stingy man hurries after riches, and doesn't know that poverty waits for him.

Proverb 28:22 NHEB

NOTES

Why have Troubles and Worries

If we fill our hours with regrets over the failures of yesterday, and with worries over the problems of tomorrow, we have no today in which to be thankful.

ANONYMOUS

❧

Therefore don't be anxious for tomorrow, for tomorrow will be anxious for itself. Each day's own evil is sufficient.

Matthew 6:34 WEB

Blessed be the God and Father of our Lord Jesus Christ, the Father of mercies and God of all comfort; who comforts us in all our affliction, that we may be able to comfort those who are in any affliction, through the comfort with which we ourselves are comforted by God.

2 Corinthians 1:3-4 WEB

We are pressed on every side, yet not crushed; perplexed, yet not to despair; pursued, yet not forsaken; struck down, yet not destroyed.

2 Corinthians 4:8-9 WEB

Cast all your worries on him, because he cares for you.

1 Peter 5:7 NHEB

Don't let your heart be troubled. Believe in God. Believe also in me.

John 14:1 WEB

In nothing be anxious, but in everything, by prayer and petition with thanksgiving, let your requests be made known to God. And the peace of God, which surpasses all understanding, will guard your hearts and your thoughts in Christ Jesus.

Philippians 4:6-7 NHEB

My God will supply every need of yours according to his riches in glory in Christ Jesus.

Philippians 4:19 NHEB

There remains therefore a Sabbath rest for the people of God. For he who has entered into his rest has himself also rested from his works, as God did from his.

Hebrews 4:9-10 WEB

For we do not have a high priest who cannot be touched with the feeling of our infirmities, but one who has been in all points tempted like we are, yet without sin. Let us therefore draw near with boldness to the throne of grace, that we may receive mercy, and may find grace for help in time of need.

Hebrews 4:15-16 NHEB

And let the peace of Christ rule in your hearts, to which also you were called in one body; and be thankful.

Colossians 3:15 NHEB

We know that all things work together for good for those who love God, to those who are called according to his purpose.

Romans 8:28 NHEB

For the mind of the flesh is death, but the mind of the Spirit is life and peace.

Romans 8:6 NHEB

For I consider that the sufferings of this present time are not worthy to be compared with the glory which will be revealed toward us.

Romans 8:18 NHEB

Peace I leave for you; my peace I give to you. Not in the way that the world gives, do I give to you. Do not let your heart be troubled, and let it not fear.

John 14:27 CPDV

These things I have spoken to you, so that my joy may be in you, and your joy may be fulfilled.

John 15:11 CPDV

Come to me, all you who labor and have been burdened, and I will refresh you.

Matthew 11:28 CPDV

These things I have spoken to you, so that you may have peace in me. In the world, you will have difficulties. But have confidence: I have overcome the world.

John 16:33 CPDV

And the Lord responded by saying to her: "Martha, Martha, you are anxious and troubled over many things. And yet only one thing is necessary. Mary has chosen the best portion, and it shall not be taken away from her."

Luke 10:41-42 CPDV

"And which of you, by being anxious, can add one cubit to his height? And why are you anxious about clothing? Consider the lilies of the field how they grow. They do not toil, neither do they spin.

Matthew 6:27-28 NHEB

In whom we have boldness in confidence through our faith in Him.

Ephesians 3:12 NHEB

I will give thanks to the LORD according to his righteousness, and will sing praise to the name of the LORD Most High.

Psalm 7:17 NHEB

The LORD will also be a refuge for the oppressed, a refuge in times of trouble. Those who know your name will put their trust in you, for you, LORD, have not forsaken those who seek you.

Psalm 9:9-10 NHEB

The LORD is my rock, my fortress, and my deliverer; my God, my rock, in whom I take refuge; my shield, and the horn of my salvation, my high tower.

Psalm 18:2 NHEB

In my distress I called on the LORD, and cried to my God. He heard my voice out of his temple. My cry before him came into his ears.

Psalm 18:6 NHEB

For he has not despised nor abhorred the affliction of the afflicted, neither has he hidden his face from him; but when he cried to him, he heard.

Psalm 22:24 NHEB

For in the day of trouble he will keep me secretly in his pavilion. In the covert of his tabernacle he will hide me. He will lift me up on a rock.

Psalm 27:5 NHEB

The LORD is my strength and my shield. My heart has trusted in him, and I am helped. Therefore my heart greatly rejoices. With my song I will thank him.

Psalm 28:7 NHEB

Oh love the LORD, all you his holy ones! The LORD preserves the faithful, and fully recompenses him who behaves arrogantly. Be strong, and let your heart take courage, all you who hope in the LORD.

Psalm 31:23-24 NHEB

You are my hiding place. You will preserve me from trouble. You will surround me with songs of deliverance. Selah.

Psalm 32:7 NHEB

Oh fear the LORD, you his holy ones, for there is no lack with those who fear him.

Psalm 34:9 NHEB

They cried, and the LORD hears, and delivers them out of all their troubles.

Psalm 34:17 NHEB

But the salvation of the righteous is from the LORD. He is their stronghold in the time of trouble.

Psalm 37:39 NHEB

Blessed is he who considers the poor. The LORD will deliver him in the day of evil.

Psalm 41:1 NHEB

Why are you in despair, my soul? Why are you disturbed within me? Hope in God! For I shall still praise him, the saving help of my countenance, and my God.

Psalm 42:11 NHEB

God is our refuge and strength, a very present help in trouble. Therefore we won't be afraid, though the earth changes, though the mountains are shaken into the heart of the seas; though its waters roar and are troubled, though the mountains tremble with their swelling. Selah.

Psalm 46:1-3 NHEB

All the earth will worship you, and will sing to you; they will sing to your name." Selah.

Psalm 66:4 NHEB

"Kings of armies flee! They flee!" She who waits at home divides the spoil, while you sleep among the campfires, the wings of a dove sheathed with silver, her feathers with shining gold.

Psalm 68:12-13 NHEB

You, who have shown us many and bitter troubles, you will let me live. You will bring us up again from the depths of the earth.

Psalm 71:20 NHEB

My flesh and my heart fails, but God is the strength of my heart and my portion forever.

Psalm 73:26 NHEB

All nations you have made will come and worship before you, Lord. They shall glorify your name.

Psalm 86:9 NHEB

No evil shall overtake you; no plague shall come near your dwelling. For he will put his angels in charge of you, to guard you in all your ways.

Psalm 91:10-11 NHEB

He will call on me, and I will answer him. I will be with him in trouble. I will deliver him, and honor him. I will satisfy him with long life, and show him my salvation."

Psalm 91:15-16 NHEB

Oh come, let's worship and bow down. Let's kneel before the LORD, our Maker, for he is our God. We are the people of his pasture, and the sheep in his care. Today, oh that you would hear his voice!

Psalm 95:6-7 NHEB

Exalt the LORD, our God. Worship at his holy hill, for the LORD, our God, is holy!

Psalm 99:9 NHEB

Those who sow in tears will reap in joy. He who goes out weeping, carrying seed for sowing, will certainly come again with joy, carrying his sheaves.

Psalm 126:5-6 NHEB

The LORD opens the eyes of the blind. The LORD raises up those who are bowed down. The LORD loves the righteous.

Psalm 146:8 NHEB

A righteous person is delivered out of trouble, and the wicked takes his place.

Proverb 11:8 NHEB

An evil man is trapped by sinfulness of lips, but the righteous shall come out of trouble.

Proverbs 12:13 NHEB

In the house of the righteous is much treasure, but the income of the wicked brings trouble.

Proverbs 15:6 NHEB

Better is little, with the fear of the LORD, than great treasure with trouble.

Proverb 15:16 NHEB

Confidence in someone unfaithful in time of trouble is like a bad tooth, or a lame foot.

Proverbs 25:19 NHEB

NOTES

He sends His Angels
and The Holy Spirit

There are more things in heaven and earth,
Horatio, than are dreamt of in your philosophy.

WILLIAM SHAKESPEARE

✤

For I am persuaded, that neither death, nor life, nor angels, nor principalities, nor things present, nor things to come, nor powers, nor height, nor depth, nor any other created thing, will be able to separate us from the love of God, which is in Christ Jesus our Lord.

Romans 8:38-39 WEB

Let no one rob you of your prize by a voluntary humility and worshiping of the angels, dwelling in the things which he has not seen, vainly puffed up by his fleshly mind.

Colossians 2:18 WEB

For there stood by me this night an angel, belonging to the God whose I am and whom I serve.

Acts 27:23 WEB

Now he who made us for this very thing is God, who also gave to us the down payment of the Spirit.

2 Corinthians 5:5 WEB

And behold, an Angel of the Lord stood near, and a light shined forth in the cell. And tapping Peter on the side, he awakened him, saying, "Rise up, quickly." And the chains fell from his hands.

Acts 12:7 CPDV

And Peter, returning to himself, said: "Now I know, truly, that the Lord sent his Angel, and that he rescued me from the hand of Herod and from all that the people of the Jews were anticipating."

Acts 12:11 CPDV

But you have come to Mount Zion, and to the city of the living God, the heavenly Jerusalem, and to innumerable multitudes of angels.

Hebrews 12:22 WEB

But which of the angels has he told at any time, "Sit at my right hand, until I make your enemies the footstool of your feet?" Aren't they all serving spirits, sent out to do service for the sake of those who will inherit salvation?

Hebrews 1:13-14 WEB

For our citizenship is in heaven, from where we also wait for a Savior, the Lord Jesus Christ, who will change the body of our humiliation to be conformed to the body of his glory, according to the working by which he is able even to subject all things to himself.

Philippians 3:20-21 WEB

Then the devil left him. And behold, Angels approached and ministered to him.

Matthew 4:11 CPDV

See to it that you do not despise even one of these little ones. For I say to you, that their Angels in heaven continually look upon the face of my Father, who is in heaven.

Matthew 18:10 CPDV

"Even so, I tell you, there is joy in the presence of the angels of God over one sinner repenting."

Luke 15:10 WEB

The beggar died, and he was carried away by the angels to Abraham's bosom. The rich man also died, and was buried.

Luke 16:22 WEB

An angel from heaven appeared to him, strengthening him.

Luke 22:43 WEB

Now at times an Angel of the Lord would descend into the pool, and so the water was moved. And whoever descended first into the pool, after the motion of the water, he was healed of whatever infirmity held him.

John 5:4 CPDV

Behold, an angel of the Lord stood by them, and the glory of the Lord shone around them, and they were terrified. The angel said to them, "Don't be afraid, for behold, I bring you good news of great joy which will be to all the people."

Luke 2:9-10 WEB

He who has an ear, let him hear what the Spirit says to the churches." After these things I looked and saw a door opened in heaven, and the first voice that I heard, like a trumpet speaking with me, was one saying, "Come up here, and I will show you the things which must happen after this." Immediately I was in the Spirit. Behold, there was a throne set in heaven, and one sitting on the throne.

Revelations 3:22- 4:1-2 NHEB

I tell you that even so there will be more joy in heaven over one sinner who repents, than over ninety-nine righteous people who need no repentance.

Luke 15:7 NHEB

The angel answered him, "I am Gabriel, who stands in the presence of God. I was sent to speak to you, and to bring you this good news.

Luke 1:19 WEB

The angel said to her, "Don't be afraid, Mary, for you have found favor with God."

Luke 1:30 WEB

But one has somewhere testified, saying, "What is man, that you think of him? Or the son of man, that you care for him? You made him a little lower than the angels. You crowned him with glory and honor."

Hebrews 2:6-7 NHEB

And the Angel said to them: "Do not be afraid. For, behold, I proclaim to you a great joy, which will be for all the people."

Luke 2:10 CPDV

But I say to you: Everyone who will have confessed me before men, the Son of man will also confess him before the Angels of God.

Luke 12:8 CPDV

Having become so much better than the angels, as he has inherited a more excellent name than they have.

Hebrews 1:14 NHEB

I saw an angel coming down out of heaven, having the key of the abyss and a great chain in his hand.

Revelation 20:1 NHEB

At about the ninth hour of the day, he clearly saw in a vision an angel of God coming to him, and saying to him, "Cornelius!" He, fastening his eyes on him, and being frightened, said, "What is it, Lord?" He said to him, "Your prayers and your gifts to the needy have gone up for a memorial before God.

Acts 10:3-4 NHEB

He who believes in me, as the Scripture has said, from within him will flow rivers of living water." But he said this about the Spirit, which those believing in him were to receive. For the Spirit was not yet given, because Jesus was not yet glorified.

John 7:38-39 NHEB

If you then, being evil, know how to give good gifts to your children, how much more will your heavenly Father give the Holy Spirit to those who ask him?"

Luke 11:13 WEB

Christ redeemed us from the curse of the law, having become a curse for us. For it is written, "Cursed is everyone who hangs on a tree," that the blessing of Abraham might come on the Gentiles through Christ Jesus; that we might receive the promise of the Spirit through faith.

Galatians 3:13-14 NHEB

For God's Kingdom is not eating and drinking, but righteousness, peace, and joy in the Holy Spirit.

Romans 14:17 WEB

He carried me away in the Spirit to a great and high mountain, and showed me the holy city, Jerusalem, coming down out of heaven from God.

Revelation 21:10 NHEB

For you didn't receive the spirit of bondage again to fear, but you received the Spirit of adoption, by whom we cry, "Abba! Father!"

Romans 8:15 WEB

But whoever drinks of the water that I will give him will never thirst again; but the water that I will give him will become in him a well of water springing up to eternal life."

John 4:14 NHEB

However when he, the Spirit of truth, has come, he will guide you into all truth, for he will not speak from himself; but whatever he hears, he will speak. He will declare to you things that are coming.

John 16:13 NHEB

I will pray to the Father, and he will give you another Counselor, that he may be with you forever— the Spirit of truth, whom the world cannot receive; for it does not see him, neither knows him. You know him, for he lives with you, and will be in you. I will not leave you orphans. I will come to you.

John 14:16-18 NHEB

And hope doesn't disappoint us, because God's love has been poured out into our hearts through the Holy Spirit who was given to us.

Romans 5:5 WEB

As for you, the anointing which you received from him remains in you, and you don't need for anyone to teach you. But as his anointing teaches you concerning all things, and is true, and is no lie, and even as it taught you, you will remain in him.

1 John 2:27 WEB

In the same way, the Spirit also helps our weaknesses, for we don't know how to pray as we ought. But the Spirit himself makes intercession for us with groanings which can't be uttered. He who searches the hearts knows what is on the Spirit's mind, because he makes intercession for the saints according to God.

Romans 8:26-27 WEB

Indeed, I baptize you with water for repentance, but he who will come after me is more powerful than me. I am not worthy to carry his shoes. He will baptize you with the fire of the Holy Spirit.

Matthew 3:11 CPDV

When they had prayed, the place was shaken where they were gathered together. They were all filled with the Holy Spirit, and they spoke the word of God with boldness.

Acts 4:31 NHEB

Peter said to them, "Repent, and be baptized, every one of you, in the name of Jesus Christ for the forgiveness of your sins, and you will receive the gift of the Holy Spirit. For to you is the promise, and to your children, and to all who are far off, even as many as the Lord our God will call to himself."

Acts 2:38-39 NHEB

Nevertheless I tell you the truth: It is to your advantage that I go away, for if I do not go away, the Counselor won't come to you. But if I go, I will send him to you. When he has come, he will convict the world about sin, about righteousness, and about judgment; about sin, because they do not believe in me. However when he, the Spirit of truth, has come, he will guide you into all truth, for he will not speak from himself; but whatever he hears, he will speak. He will declare to you things that are coming. He will glorify me, for he will take from what is mine, and will declare it to you.

John 16:7-9, 13-14 NHEB

While Peter was still speaking these words, the Holy Spirit fell on all those who heard the word. They of the circumcision who believed were amazed, as many as came with Peter, because the gift of the Holy Spirit was also poured out on the Gentiles.

Acts 10:44-45 NHEB

For as many as are led by the Spirit of God, these are children of God. For you didn't receive the spirit of bondage again to fear, but you received the Spirit of adoption, by whom we cry, "Abba! Father!" The Spirit himself testifies with our spirit that we are children of God.

Romans 8:14-16 WEB

For the mind of the flesh is death, but the mind of the Spirit is life and peace.

Romans 8:6 WEB

All the angels were standing around the throne, the elders, and the four living creatures; and they fell on their faces before the throne, and worshiped God, saying, "Amen! Blessing, glory, wisdom, thanksgiving, honor, power, and might, be to our God forever and ever! Amen."

Revelation 7:11-12 NHEB

Again, when he brings in the firstborn into the world he says, "Let all the angels of God worship him." Of the angels he says, "Who makes his angels winds, and his servants a flame of fire."

Hebrews 1:6-7 NHEB

Are not they all serving spirits, sent out to do service for the sake of those who will inherit salvation?

Hebrews 1:14 NHEB

Do not forget to show hospitality to strangers, for in doing so; some have entertained angels without knowing it.

Hebrews 13:2 NHEB

To them it was revealed, that they served not to themselves, but to you, in these things, which now have been announced to you through those who preached the Good News to you by the Holy Spirit sent out from heaven; which things angels desire to look into.

1 Peter 1:12 WEB

But to us, God revealed them through the Spirit. For the Spirit searches all things, yes, the deep things of God.

1 Corinthians 2:10 WEB

For it is written that he has given his Angels charge over you, so that they may guard you.

Luke 4:10 CPDV

And immediately the Spirit prompted him into the desert. And he was in the desert for forty days and forty nights. And he was tempted by Satan. And he was with the wild animals, and the Angels ministered to him.

Mark 1:12-13 CPDV

Now in the sixth month, the angel Gabriel was sent from God to a city of Galilee, named Nazareth, to a virgin pledged to be married to a man whose name was Joseph, of the house of David. The virgin's name was Mary. Having come in, the angel said to her, "Rejoice, you highly favored one! The Lord is with you! "But when she saw him, she was greatly troubled at the saying, and considered what kind of salutation this might be. The angel said to her, "Do not be afraid, Mary, for you have found favor with God. Behold, you will conceive in your womb, and bring forth a son, and will call his name 'Jesus.'

Luke 1:26-31 NHEB

For the creation was subjected to vanity, not of its own will, but because of him who subjected it, in hope that the creation itself also will be delivered from the bondage of decay into the liberty of the glory of the children of God. For we know that the whole creation groans and travails in pain together until now. Not only so, but ourselves also, who have the first fruits of the Spirit, even we ourselves groan within ourselves, waiting for adoption, the redemption of our body.

Romans 8:20-23 NHEB

For he will put his angels in charge of you, to guard you in all your ways.

Psalm 91:11 NHEB

NOTES

He is the Author of Salvation

❧

For my eyes have seen your salvation, which you have prepared before the face of all peoples.

Luke 2:30-31 CPDV

There is salvation in none other, for neither is there any other name
under heaven, that is given among men, by which we must be saved!"

Acts 4:12 WEB

Brothers, children of the stock of Abraham, and those among you
who fear God, the word of this salvation is sent out to us.

Acts 13:26 WEB

They said, "Believe in the Lord Jesus Christ, and you will be saved, you and your household."

Acts 16:31 NHEB

Jesus said to him: "I am the Way, and the Truth, and the Life. No one comes to the Father, except through me."

John 14:6 CPDV

For I am not ashamed of the Good News of Christ, for it is the power of God for salvation for everyone who believes; for the Jew first, and also for the Greek.

Romans 1:16 WEB

That if you will confess with your mouth that Jesus is Lord, and believe in your heart that God raised him from the dead, you will be saved. For with the heart, one believes unto righteousness; and with the mouth confession is made unto salvation.

Romans 10:9-10 WEB

Do this; knowing the time, that it is already time for you to awaken out of sleep, for salvation is now nearer to us than when we first believed.

Romans 13:11 WEB

And take the helmet of salvation, and the sword of the Spirit, which is the spoken word of God.

Ephesians 6:17 NHEB

And perseverance, proven character; and proven character, hope.

Romans 5:4 WEB

For the grace of God has appeared, bringing salvation to all men.

Titus 2:11 WEB

For those who sleep, sleep in the night, and those who are drunk are drunk in the night. But let us, since we belong to the day, be sober, putting on the breastplate of faith and love, and, for a helmet, the hope of salvation.

1 Thessalonians 5:7-8 WEB

And, from your infancy, you have known the Sacred Scriptures, which are able to instruct you toward salvation, through the faith which is in Christ Jesus.

2 Timothy 3:15 CPDV

Receiving the result of your faith, the salvation of your souls.

1 Peter 1:9 WEB

To an incorruptible and undefiled inheritance that does not fade away, reserved in Heaven for you, who by the power of God are guarded through faith for a salvation ready to be revealed in the last time.

1 Peter 1:4-5 NHEB

For he says, "At an acceptable time I listened to you, in a day of salvation I helped you." Behold, now is the acceptable time. Behold, now is the day of salvation.

2 Corinthians 6:2 NHEB

So Christ also, having been offered once to bear the sins of many, will appear a second time, without sin, to those who are eagerly waiting for him for salvation.

Hebrews 9:28 WEB

They shouted with a loud voice, saying, "Salvation be to our God, who sits on the throne, and to the Lamb!"

Revelation 7:10 NHEB

For the Lord himself will descend from heaven with a shout, with the voice of the archangel, and with God's trumpet. The dead in Christ will rise first, then we who are alive, who are left, will be caught up together with them in the clouds, to meet the Lord in the air. So we will be with the Lord forever. Therefore comfort one another with these words.

1 Thessalonians 4:16-18 WEB

But he who endures to the end, the same will be saved.

Matthew 24:13 WEB

Jesus responded and said to him, "Amen, amen, I say to you, unless one has been reborn anew, he is not able to see the kingdom of God." Nicodemus said to him: "How can a man be born when he is old? Surely, he cannot enter a second time into his mother's womb to be reborn?" Jesus responded: "Amen, amen, I say to you, unless one has been reborn by water and the Holy Spirit, he is not able to enter into the kingdom of God. What is born of the flesh is flesh, and what is born of the Spirit is spirit. You should not be amazed that I said to you: You must be born anew.

John 3:3-7 CPDV

Yet whoever did accept him, those who believed in his name, he gave them the power to become the sons of God. These are born, not of blood, nor of the will of flesh, nor of the will of man, but of God.

John 1:12-13 CPDV

You were made alive when you were dead in transgressions and sins.

Ephesians 2:1 WEB

For this is good and acceptable in the sight of God our Savior; who desires all people to be saved and come to full knowledge of the truth.

1 Timothy 2:3-4 WEB

This saying is faithful and worthy of all acceptance. For to this end we both labor and strive, because we have set our trust in the living God, who is the Savior of all men, especially of those who believe.

1 Timothy 4:9-10 NHEB

You were dead through your trespasses and the uncircumcision of your flesh. He made you alive together with him, having forgiven us all our trespasses.

Colossians 2:13 WEB

But the free gift is not like the trespass. For if by the trespass of the one the many died, much more did the grace of God, and the gift by the grace of the one man, Jesus Christ, abound to the many.

Romans 5:15 NHEB

For I am persuaded, that neither death, nor life nor angels, nor principalities, nor things to come, nor powers, nor height, nor depth, nor any other created thing, will be able to separate us from the love of God, which is in Christ Jesus our Lord.

Romans 8:38-39 NHEB

Salvation belongs to the LORD. Your blessing be on your people. Selah.

Psalm 3:8 NHEB

Guide me in your truth, and teach me, for you are the God of my salvation, I wait for you all day long.

Psalm 25:5 NHEB

The LORD is my light and my salvation. Whom shall I fear? The LORD is the strength of my life. Of whom shall I be afraid?

Psalm 27:1 NHEB

My soul shall be joyful in the LORD. It shall rejoice in his salvation.

Psalm 35:9 NHEB

Restore to me the joy of your salvation. Uphold me with a willing spirit.

Psalm 51:12 NHEB

My soul rests in God alone. My salvation is from him. He alone is my rock and my salvation, my fortress—I will never be greatly shaken.

Psalm 62:1-2 NHEB

Show us your loving kindness, LORD. Grant us your salvation.

Psalm 85:7 NHEB

He will call on me, and I will answer him. I will be with him in trouble. I will deliver him, and honor him. I will satisfy him with long life, and show him my salvation."

Psalm 91:15-16 NHEB

Oh come, let's sing to the LORD. Let's shout aloud to the rock of our salvation!

Psalm 95:1 NHEB

I will take the cup of salvation, and call on the name of the LORD.

Psalm 116:13 NHEB

For the LORD takes pleasure in his people. He crowns the humble with salvation.

Psalm 149:4 NHEB

LORD, the strength of my salvation, you have covered my head in the day of battle.

Psalm 140:7 NHEB

NOTES

He is the Giver of Eternal Life

The nearer she approached the end, the plainer she seemed to hear round her the immortal symphonies of the world to come.

ANONYMOUS

❧

Most certainly, I tell you, he who believes in me has eternal life.

John 6:47 WEB

Jesus said to her, "I am the resurrection and the life. He who believes in me will still live, even if he dies. Whoever lives and believes in me will never die. Do you believe this?"

John 11:25-26 WEB

For God so loved the world, that he gave his one and only Son, that whoever believes in him should not perish, but have eternal life.

John 3:16 WEB

Don't marvel at this, for the hour comes, in which all that are in the tombs will hear his voice, and will come out; those who have done good, to the resurrection of life; and those who have done evil, to the resurrection of judgment.

John 5:28-29 WEB

In my Father's house are many homes. If it weren't so, I would have told you. I am going to prepare a place for you.

John 14:2-3 WEB

Behold, I tell you a mystery. We will not all sleep, but we will all be changed, in a moment, in the twinkling of an eye, at the last trumpet. For the trumpet will sound, and the dead will be raised incorruptible, and we will be changed. For this corruptible must put on incorruption, and this mortal must put on immortality. But when this corruptible will have put on incorruption, and this mortal will have put on immortality, then what is written will happen: "Death is swallowed up in victory." "Death, where is your victory? Death, where is your sting?"

1 Corinthians 15:51-55 NHEB

Who will change the body of our humiliation to be conformed to the body of his glory, according to the working by which he is able even to subject all things to himself?

Philippians 3:21 WEB

For since death came by man, the resurrection of the dead also came by man.

1 Corinthians 15:21 NHEB

So also is the resurrection of the dead. It is sown in corruption; it is raised in incorruption. It is sown in dishonor; it is raised in glory. It is sown in weakness; it is raised in power; It is sown a natural body; it is raised a spiritual body. There is a natural body and there is also a spiritual body.

1 Corinthians 15:42-44 NHEB

For we know that if the earthly house of our tent is dissolved, we have a building from God, a house not made with hands, eternal, in the heavens.

2 Corinthians 5:1 NHEB

And this is the promise that he hath promised us, even eternal life.

1 John 2:25 AKJV

And this is the record, that God hath given to us eternal life, and this life is in his Son.

1 John 5:11 AKJV

For the Lord himself will descend from heaven with a shout, with the voice of the archangel, and with God's trumpet. The dead in Christ will rise first, then we who are alive, who are left, will be caught up together with them in the clouds, to meet the Lord in the air. So we will be with the Lord forever.

1 Thessalonians 4:16-17 WEB

These things I have written to you who believe in the name of the Son of God, that you may know that you have eternal life, and that you may continue to believe in the name of the Son of God.

1 John 5:13 WEB

Therefore they are before the throne of God; they serve him day and night in his temple. He who sits on the throne will spread his tabernacle over them. They will hunger no more, neither thirst anymore; neither will the sun beat on them, nor any heat; for the Lamb who is in the midst of the throne shepherds them, and leads them to springs of waters of life. And God will wipe away every tear from their eyes."

Revelation 7:15-17 NHEB

He will wipe away from them every tear from their eyes. Death will be no more; neither will there be mourning, nor crying, nor pain, any more. The first things have passed away."

Revelation 21:4 NHEB

For the wages of sin is death, but the free gift of God is eternal life in Christ Jesus our Lord.

Romans 6:23 WEB

But if the Spirit of him who raised up Jesus from the dead dwells in you, he who raised up Christ Jesus from the dead will also give life to your mortal bodies through his Spirit who dwells in you.

Romans 8:11 WEB

NOTES

His Forgiveness is Divine

If we learn how to give ourselves, to forgive others, and to live with thanksgiving, we need not seek happiness —it will seek us.

ANONYMOUS

For if you will forgive men their sins, your heavenly Father also will forgive you your offenses.

Matthew 6:14 CPDV

But I say to you: Love your enemies. Do good to those who hate you. And pray for those who persecute and slander you. In this way, you shall be sons of your Father, who is in heaven.

Matthew 5:44-45 CPDV

But Jesus, hearing this, said: "It is not those who are healthy who are in need of a physician, but those who have maladies."

Matthew 9:12 CPDV

And when you stand to pray, if you hold anything against anyone, forgive them, so that your Father, who is in heaven, may also forgive you your sins. But if you will not forgive, neither will your Father, who is in heaven, forgive you your sins."

Mark 11:25-26 CPDV

Therefore "If your enemy is hungry, feed him. If he is thirsty, give him a drink; for in doing so, you will heap coals of fire on his head."

Romans 12:20 NHEB

Those who sat at the table with him began to say to themselves, "Who is this who even forgives sins?"

Luke 7:49 WEB

But love your enemies, and do good, and lend, expecting nothing back; and your reward will be great, and you will be children of the Most High; for he is kind toward the unthankful and evil. Therefore be merciful, even as your Father is also merciful. Do not judge, and you won't be judged. Do not condemn, and you won't be condemned. Forgive, and you will be forgiven. "Give, and it will be given to you: good measure, pressed down, shaken together, and running over, will be given to you. For with the same measure you measure it will be measured back to you."

Luke 6:35-38 NHEB

Be it known to you therefore, brothers, that through this man is proclaimed to you remission of sins.

Acts 13:38 NHEB

In whom we have our redemption through his blood, the forgiveness of our trespasses, according to the riches of his grace.

Ephesians 1:7 NHEB

And be kind to one another, tender hearted, forgiving each other, just as God also in Christ forgave you.

Ephesians 4:32 WEB

If we confess our sins, he is faithful and righteous to forgive us the sins, and to cleanse us from all unrighteousness.

1 John 1:9 WEB

For you will not leave my soul in Sheol, neither will you allow your holy one to see corruption.

Psalm 16:10 NHEB

As far as the east is from the west, so far has he removed our transgressions from us.

Psalm 103:12 NHEB

NOTES

His Grace becomes my Glory

There are only two ways to live your life. One is as though nothing is a miracle. The other is as though everything is a miracle.

ALBERT EINSTEIN

✣

For the LORD God is a sun and a shield. The LORD will give grace and glory. He withholds no good thing from those who walk blamelessly.

Psalm 84:11 NHEB

In this, my Father is glorified: that you should bring forth very much fruit and become my disciples.

John 15:8 CPDV

Being filled with the fruit of righteousness, which are through Jesus Christ, to the glory and praise of God.

Philippians 1:11 NHEB

This I pray, that your love may abound yet more and more in knowledge and all discernment.

Philippians 1:9 NHEB

I press on toward the goal for the prize of the high calling of God in Christ Jesus. Let us therefore, as many as are perfect, think this way. If in anything you think otherwise, God will also reveal that to you. Nevertheless, to what we have attained, to the same continue on.

Philippians 3:14-16 NHEB

Let no one deceive himself. If anyone thinks that he is wise among you in this world, let him become a fool that he may become wise.

1 Corinthians 3:18 WEB

While they themselves also, with supplication on your behalf, yearn for you by reason of the exceeding grace of God in you. Now thanks be to God for his unspeakable gift!

2 Corinthians 9:14-15 WEB

But be careful that by no means does this liberty of yours become a stumbling block to the weak.

1 Corinthians 8:9 WEB

The grace of the Lord Jesus Christ, the love of God, and the fellowship of the Holy Spirit, be with you all.

2 Corinthians 13:14 WEB

For our boasting is this: the testimony of our conscience, that in holiness and sincerity of God, not in fleshly wisdom but in the grace of God we behaved ourselves in the world, and more abundantly toward you.

2 Corinthians 1:12 NHEB

But by the grace of God I am what I am.

1 Corinthians 15:10 NHEB

Which has come to you; even as it is in all the world and is bearing fruit and growing, as it does in you also, since the day you heard and knew the grace of God in truth.

Colossians 1:6 NHEB

Finally then, brothers, we beg and exhort you in the Lord Jesus, that as you received from us how you ought to walk and to please God, that you abound more and more.

1 Thessalonians 4:1 WEB

We are bound to always give thanks to God for you, brothers, even as it is appropriate, because your faith grows exceedingly, and the love of each and every one of you towards one another abounds.

2 Thessalonians 1:3 NHEB

Who by the power of God are guarded through faith for a salvation ready to be revealed in the last time.

1 Peter 1:5 NHEB

But we believe that we are saved through the grace of the Lord Jesus, just as they are.

Acts 15:11 NHEB

And the God of peace will quickly crush Satan under your feet. The grace of our Lord Jesus Christ be with you.

Romans 16:20 WEB

I do not make void the grace of God.

Galatians 2:21 NHEB

Let us therefore draw near with boldness to the throne of grace, that we may receive mercy, and may find grace for help in time of need.

Hebrew 4:16 NHEB

That the name of our Lord Jesus may be glorified in you, and you in him, according to the grace of our God and the Lord Jesus Christ.

2 Thessalonians 1:12 NHEB

For the grace of God that bringeth salvation hath appeared to all men.

Titus 2:11 AKJV

But has now been revealed by the appearing of our Savior, Christ Jesus, who abolished death, and brought life and immortality to light through the Good News.

2 Timothy 1:10 NHEB

Grace be with all those who love our Lord Jesus Christ with incorruptible love.

Ephesians 6:24 NHEB

NOTES

He wipes away all Guilt and Shame

*I have resolved never to do anything which I should
be afraid to do if it were the last hour of life.*

ANONYMOUS

✤

If we confess our sins, he is faithful and righteous to forgive us the
sins, and to cleanse us from all unrighteousness.

1 John 1:9 WEB

Little children, let us not love in word only, neither with the tongue
only, but in deed and truth. And by this we will know that we are of
the truth, and persuade our heart before him, because if our heart
condemns us, God is greater than our heart, and knows all things.
Beloved, if our hearts do not condemn us, we have boldness toward
God.

1 John 3:18-21 NHEB

I write to you, little children, because your sins are forgiven you for his name's sake.

1 John 2:12 WEB

But if we walk in the light, as he is in the light, we have fellowship with one another, and the blood of Jesus, his Son, cleanses us from all sin.

1 John 1:7 WEB

Therefore if anyone is in Christ, he is a new creation. The old things have passed away. Behold, all things have become new.

2 Corinthians 5:17 WEB

I do not write these things to shame you, but to admonish you as my beloved children. I beg you therefore, be imitators of me.

1 Corinthians 4:14, 16 NHEB

For the Scripture says, "Whoever believes in him will not be disappointed.

Romans 10:11 WEB

And hope doesn't disappoint us, because God's love has been poured out into our hearts through the Holy Spirit who was given to us.

Romans 5:5 WEB

There is therefore now no condemnation to those who are in Christ Jesus, who don't walk according to the flesh, but according to the Spirit.

Romans 8:1 WEB

Even as it is written, "Behold, I lay in Zion a stumbling stone and a rock that will make them fall; and no one who believes in him will be put to shame.

Romans 9:33 NHEB

Do your best to present yourself approved by God, a workman who does not need to be ashamed, properly handling the Word of Truth.

2 Timothy 2:15 NHEB

But if one of you suffers for being a Christian, let him not be ashamed; but let him glorify God in this name.

1 Peter 4:16 NHEB

Looking to Jesus, the author and finisher of our faith, who for the joy that was set before him endured the cross, disregarding its shame, and has sat down at the right hand of the throne of God.

Hebrew 12:2 NHEB

The LORD redeems the soul of his servants. None of those who take refuge in him shall be condemned.

Psalm 34:22 NHEB

As far as the east is from the west, so far has he removed our transgressions from us.

Psalm 103:12 NHEB

I cling to your statutes, LORD. Do not let me be disappointed.

Psalm 119:31 NHEB

Then I wouldn't be disappointed, when I consider all of your commandments.

Psalm 119:6 NHEB

Let my heart be blameless toward your decrees, that I may not be disappointed.

Psalm 119:80 NHEB

NOTES

He is The One True Comforter

It was decided long before you became,
that you would become.

*V A H*AYS

❖

"These things I have spoken to you, so that you may have peace in me. In the world, you will have difficulties. But have confidence: I have overcome the world."

John 16:33 CPDV

For as the sufferings of Christ abound to us, even so our comfort also abounds through Christ.

2 Corinthians 1:5 WEB

"Come to me, all you who labor and are heavily burdened, and I will give you rest."

Mathew 11:28 WEB

Great is my boldness of speech toward you. Great is my boasting on your behalf. I am filled with comfort. I overflow with joy in all our affliction.

> 2 Corinthians 7:4 WEB

For this cause, brothers, we were comforted over you in all our distress and affliction through your faith.

> 1 Thessalonians 3:7 NHEB

Now our Lord Jesus Christ himself, and God our Father, who loved us and gave us eternal comfort and good hope through grace, comfort your hearts and establish you in every good work and word.

> 2 Thessalonians 2:16-17 WEB

The LORD will also be a refuge for the oppressed, a refuge in times of trouble.

> Psalm 9:9 NHEB

The LORD is my rock, my fortress, and my deliverer; my God, my rock, in whom I take refuge; my shield, and the horn of my salvation, my high tower.

> Psalm 18:2 NHEB

For he has not despised nor abhorred the affliction of the afflicted, neither has he hidden his face from him; but when he cried to him, he heard.

> Psalm 22:24 NHEB

The eyes of the LORD are toward the righteous. His ears listen to their cry.

> Psalm 34:15 NHEB

A man's goings are established by the LORD. He delights in his way. Though he stumble, he shall not fall, for the LORD holds him up with his hand.

Psalm 37:23-24 NHEB

But the salvation of the righteous is from the LORD. He is their stronghold in the time of trouble.

Psalm 37:39 NHEB

God is our refuge and strength, a very present help in trouble. Therefore we won't be afraid, though the earth changes, though the mountains are shaken into the heart of the seas; though its waters roar and are troubled, though the mountains tremble with their swelling. Selah.

Psalm 46:1-3 NHEB

Cast your burden on the LORD, and he will sustain you. He will never allow the righteous to be moved.

Psalm 55:22 NHEB

Though I walk in the midst of trouble, you will revive me. You will stretch forth your hand against the wrath of my enemies. Your right hand will save me.

Psalm 138:7 NHEB

Voletta Ann Hays

NOTES

When all else fails - Pray

You are not a reservoir with a limited amount of resources. You are a channel attached to unlimited divine resources.

ANONYMOUS

And he said to them," When you pray, say, Our Father which are in heaven, Hallowed be your name. Your kingdom come. Your will be done, as in heaven, so in earth. Give us day by day our daily bread. And forgive us our sins; for we also forgive every one that is indebted to us. And lead us not into temptation; but deliver us from evil."

Luke 11:2-4 AKJV

For this reason, I say to you, all things whatsoever that you ask for when praying: believe that you will receive them, and they will happen for you.

Mark 11:24 CPDV

For they heard them speaking in other languages and magnifying God.

Acts 10:46 WEB

And he said, 'Cornelius, your prayer is heard, and your gifts to the needy are remembered in the sight of God.

Acts 10:31 NHEB

But I say to you: Love your enemies. Do good to those who hate you. And pray for those who persecute and slander you.

Matthew 5:44 CPDV

He also spoke a parable to them that they must always pray, and not give up.

Luke 18:1 WEB

"Ask, and it will be given you. Seek, and you will find. Knock, and it will be opened for you. For everyone who asks receives. He who seeks finds. To him who knocks it will be opened."

Matthew 7:7-8 WEB

All things, whatever you ask in prayer, believing, you will receive."

Matthew 21:22 WEB

But you, when you pray, enter into your room, and having shut the door, pray to your Father in secret, and your Father, who sees in secret, will repay you.

Matthew 6:6 CPDV

Therefore, do not choose to imitate them. For your Father knows what your needs may be, even before you ask him.

Matthew 6:8 CPDV

If you then, being evil, know how to give good gifts to your children, how much more will your Father who is in heaven give good things to those who ask him!

Matthew 7:11 WEB

This is the boldness which we have toward him, that, if we ask anything according to his will, he listens to us. And if we know that he listens to us, whatever we ask, we know that we have the petitions which we have asked of him.

1 John 5:14-15 WEB

Confess your offenses to one another, and pray for one another, that you may be healed. The insistent prayer of a righteous person is powerfully effective.

James 5:16 WEB

And whatever we ask, we receive from him, because we keep his commandments and do the things that are pleasing in his sight.

1 John 3:22 WEB

And so I say to you: Ask, and it shall be given to you. Seek, and you shall find. Knock, and it shall be opened to you.

Luke 11:9 CPDV

And whatever you shall ask the Father in my name, that I will do, so that the Father may be glorified in the Son. If you shall ask anything of me in my name, that I will do.

John 14:13-14 CPDV

If you abide in me, and my words abide in you, then you may ask for whatever you will, and it shall be done for you.

John 15:7 CPDV

Therefore you now have sorrow, but I will see you again, and your heart will rejoice, and no one will take your joy away from you. "In that day you will ask me no questions. Truly I tell you, whatever you may ask of the Father in my name, he will give it to you. Until now, you have asked nothing in my name. Ask, and you will receive, that your joy may be made full.

John 16:22-24 NHEB

And in praying, do not use vain repetitions, as the Gentiles do; for they think that they will be heard for their much speaking. Therefore do not be like them, for your Father knows what things you need, before you ask him.

Matthew 6:7-8 NHEB

He, fastening his eyes on him, and being frightened, said, "What is it, Lord?" He said to him, "Your prayers and your gifts to the needy have gone up for a memorial before God.

Acts 10:4 WEB

Peter therefore was kept in the prison, but constant prayer was made by the assembly to God for him.

Acts 12:5 WEB

While they themselves also, with supplication on your behalf, yearn for you by reason of the exceeding grace of God in you.

2 Corinthians 9:14 NHEB

For this reason, I say to you, all things whatsoever that you ask for when praying: believe that you will receive them, and they will happen for you.

Mark 11:24 CPDV

I pray for them. I don't pray for the world, but for those whom you have given me, for they are yours.

John 17:9 WEB

Rejoice always. Pray without ceasing.

1 Thessalonians 5:16-17 WEB

Is any among you suffering? Let him pray. Is any cheerful? Let him sing praises.

James 5:13 WEB

And take the helmet of salvation, and the sword of the Spirit, which is the spoken word of God; with all prayer and requests, praying at all times in the Spirit, and being watchful to this end in all perseverance and requests for all the saints.

Ephesians 6:17-18 NHEB

One God and Father of all, who is over all, and through all, and in all.

Ephesians 4:6 NHEB

This I pray, that your love may abound yet more and more in knowledge and all discernment.

Philippians 1:9 WEB

For the eyes of the Lord are on the righteous, and his ears open to their prayer; but the face of the Lord is against those who do evil."

1 Peter 3:12 WEB

Rejoicing in hope; enduring in troubles; continuing steadfastly in prayer.

Romans 12:12 WEB

Listen to the voice of my cry, my King and my God; for to you do I pray.

Psalm 5:2 NHEB

LORD, in the morning you shall hear my voice. In the morning I will lay my requests before you, and will watch expectantly.

Psalm 5:3 NHEB

The LORD has heard my supplication. The LORD accepts my prayer.

Psalm 6:9 NHEB

They cried, and the LORD hears, and delivers them out of all their troubles.

Psalm 34:17 NHEB

Evening, morning, and at noon, I will cry out in distress. He will hear my voice.

Psalm 55:17 NHEB

You who hear prayer, to you all men will come.

Psalm 65:2 NHEB

But as for me, my prayer is to you, LORD, in an acceptable time. God, in the abundance of your loving kindness, answer me in the truth of your salvation.

Psalm 69:13 NHEB

Let my prayer enter into your presence. Turn your ear to my cry.

Psalm 88:2 NHEB

I will say of the LORD, "He is my refuge and my fortress; my God, in whom I trust."

Psalm 91:2 NHEB

He will call on me, and I will answer him. I will be with him in trouble. I will deliver him, and honor him.

Psalm 91:15 NHEB

The LORD is near to all those who call on him, to all who call on him in truth. He will fulfill the desire of those who fear him. He also will hear their cry, and will save them.

Psalm 145:18-19 NHEB

The LORD is far from the wicked, but he hears the prayer of the righteous.

Proverb 15:29 NHEB

Pray like this: 'Our Father in heaven, hallowed be your name. Let your Kingdom come. Let your will be done, on earth as it is in heaven. Give us today our daily bread. And forgive us our debts, as we also forgive our debtors. Let us not come into temptation, but deliver us from the evil one. [For yours is the kingdom, the power, and the glory forever. Amen.]'

Matthew 6:9-13 NHEB

NOTES

Heaven, our Home Sweet Home

*Lift your eyes to the heavens and
hear your soul rejoice.*

V A HAYS

✤

"Don't lay up treasures for yourselves on the earth, where moth and rust consume, and where thieves break through and steal; but lay up for yourselves treasures in heaven, where neither moth nor rust consume, and where thieves don't break through and steal; for where your treasure is, there your heart will be also."

Matthew 6:19-21 WEB

But when Jesus saw it, he was moved with indignation, and said to them, "Allow the little children to come to me! Don't forbid them, for God's Kingdom belongs to such as these."

Mark 10:14 WEB

"Do not let your heart be troubled. You believe in God. Believe in me also. In my Father's house, there are many dwelling places. If there were not, I would have told you. For I go to prepare a place for you. And if I go and prepare a place for you, I will return again, and then I will take you to myself, so that where I am, you also may be. And you know where I am going. And you know the way." Jesus said to him: "I am the Way, and the Truth, and the Life. No one comes to the Father, except through me."

John 14:1-4, 6 CPDV

For the creation was subjected to vanity, not of its own will, but because of him who subjected it, in hope that the creation itself also will be delivered from the bondage of decay into the liberty of the glory of the children of God. For we know that the whole creation groans and travails in pain together until now. Not only so, but ourselves also, who have the first fruits of the Spirit, even we ourselves groan within ourselves, waiting for adoption, the redemption of our body.

Romans 8:20-23 NHEB

For we know that if the earthly house of our tent is dissolved, we have a building from God, a house not made with hands, eternal, in the heavens. For truly in this we groan, longing to be clothed with our habitation which is from heaven; if so be that being clothed we will not be found naked. For indeed we who are in this tent do groan, being burdened; not that we desire to be unclothed, but that we desire to be clothed, that what is mortal may be swallowed up by life. Now he who made us for this very thing is God, who also gave to us the down payment of the Spirit. Therefore, we are always confident and know that while we are at home in the body, we are absent from the Lord; for we walk by faith, not by sight. We are of good courage,

I say, and are willing rather to be absent from the body, and to be at home with the Lord.

2 Corinthians 5:1-8 NHEB

Now I say this, brothers, that flesh and blood cannot inherit the Kingdom of God; neither does corruption inherit incorruption. Behold, I a mystery. We will not all sleep, but we will all be changed, in a moment, in the twinkling of an eye, at the last trumpet. For the trumpet will sound, and the dead will be raised incorruptible, and we will be changed. For this corruptible must put on incorruption, and this mortal must put on immortality.

1 Corinthians 15:50-53 NHEB

Beloved, now we are children of God, and it is not yet revealed what we will be. We know that, when he is revealed, we will be like him; for we will see him just as he is.

1 John 3:2 NHEB

You will show me the path of life. In your presence is fullness of joy. In your right hand there are pleasures forevermore.

Psalm 16:11 NHEB

Surely goodness and loving kindness shall follow me all the days of my life, and I will dwell in the LORD's house forever.

Psalm 23:6 NHEB

NOTES

Beloved, now we are children of God, and it is not yet revealed what we will be. But we know that, when He is revealed, we will be like Him; for we will see Him just as He is.

This is our Hope!

EVERYDAY VICTIM BLAMING

CHALLENGING INSTITUTIONAL DISBELIEF AROUND
DOMESTIC & SEXUAL VIOLENCE AND ABUSE

Published by EVB Press www.evbpress.com United Kingdom

Edited by Louise Pennington

Logo designed by Ashley Hallatt

Cover designed by Lynn Schreiber

Manufactured in the United Kingdom

For permission to reproduce any material in this book contact EVB Press at

www.evbpress.com

ISBN: 978-1-910748-03-9 (paperback)

ISBN: 978-1-910748-04-6 (kindle)

Dedicated to the all the women who have supported our campaign and trusted us with their personal stories of domestic and sexual violence and abuse in hope that one day our campaign will be obsolete.

Thanks to Jo & Cath Costello, Lynn Schreiber, Katharine Edgar, Lucy Allen, Cath Andrews, Carm Bithell, Bee Jones, Gill Neill, Melissa Wilde, Ailsa Burkimsher Sadler, Portia Smart, Karen Ingala Smith, Barbara Carregonnen, Alison Boydell, Marina Strinkovsky, Cathryn Pharis, Sharon Yeoman, Rachel Wyatt and my best sister Kelly.

With special thank yous to everyone who donated their writing to this anthology